Case Studies in Elementary Science

Learning from Teachers

Ann C. Howe
North Carolina State University

Sharon E. Nichols
East Carolina University

Merrill
Prentice Hall

Upper Saddle River, New Jersey
Columbus, Ohio

Library of Congress Cataloging-in-Publication Data

Howe, Ann C.
    Case studies in elementary science : learning from teachers / Ann C. Howe, Sharon E. Nichols.—1st ed.
        p.   cm.
    Includes bibliographical references and index.
    ISBN 0-13-082467-4
        1. Science—Study and teaching (Elementary)—United States—Case studies. 2. Science teachers—United
States—Case studies. 3. Constructivism (Education)—United States—Case studies.   I. Nichols, Sharon E. II. Title.
    LB1585.3.H68   2001
    372.3'5044—dc21

                                                                                      00-028368

Vice President and Publisher: Jeffery W. Johnston
Editors: Bradley J. Potthoff and Linda Ashe Montgomery
Production Editor: Mary M. Irvin
Design Coordinator: Diane C. Lorenzo
Photo Coordinator: Carol Sykes
Text Design: Ed Horcharik/Pagination
Cover Design: Brian Huber
Cover Art: VSA Arts, John Shaw, Green Butterfly, 1996
Electronic Text Management: Marilyn Wilson Phelps, Karen Bretz, Melanie Ortega
Production Manager: Pamela D. Bennett
Director of Marketing: Kevin Flanagan
Marketing Manager: Amy June
Marketing Services Manager: Krista Groshong

This book was set in Garamond by Prentice Hall and was printed and bound by R. R. Donnelley & Sons Company. The cover was printed by Phoenix Color Corp.

Photo Credits: Anthony Magnacca/Merrill, pp. 1, 39, 107; Barbara Schwartz/Merrill, pp. 57, 109; Tom Watson/Merrill, pp. 13, 91; Todd Yarrington/Merrill, p.64.

10 9 8 7 6 5 4 3 2 1
ISBN: 0-13-082467-4

Preface

The case studies in this book are not imaginary stories constructed from a theory. All of them were written by real teachers who share their experiences of teaching science to children in real classrooms. The cases were chosen to illustrate the broad range and variety of decisions that teachers make every day as they guide learning in the classroom and interact with colleagues, administrators and parents outside of the classroom.

A *case*, as we use the term, is the original story or account written by a teacher and is the raw material for the case study. We asked the teachers to reflect on their recent science teaching experience and to write about an incident or situation that for some reason stuck in their minds, either as an example of a successful resolution of a problem or as an example of a situation that they could not resolve to their own satisfaction. The incident or episode is considered a case of a larger class; it is but one among many examples that might be chosen for study. Some teachers chose to write about an incident in the past that still troubled them rather than a more recent event.

A *case study*, sometimes called a *teaching case*, is a case that has been developed to use in instruction. Each case study in this book has a brief introduction to place it in context and is followed by questions to stimulate discussion. The value of using case studies in instruction is in the thoughtful discussion, analysis, and reflection that they stimulate and the consideration of the complexities and the ambiguities inherent in teaching science.

Each teacher who contributed to this book tried to compose a story that would engage the interest of readers and deepen their understanding of the multifaceted nature of science teaching. Some of the stories have been left just as teachers wrote them, while others have been edited to emphasize points or add details that were missing. For some cases we went back to the teachers to ask for more background, more details, or more explanation of why the decision was made as it was. In all cases, the teachers who wrote them gave permission to have them published.

The focus in all the cases is on situations and decisions that are related to teaching science. Each case deals with an important issue or dilemma that arose in elementary science teaching, and each required the teacher to make a decision or a series of decisions. Most of the cases required the writers to make decisions that were never obvious and were sometimes difficult. These cases take preservice and inservice teachers beyond the realm of rules and predetermined answers; they deal with situations that require judgment and the weighing of one value or principle against another when both are worthy and important.

The emphasis throughout the book is on the base of practical knowledge that underlies successful teaching rather than on the application of theories from education or psychology. The primary purpose is to help preservice and beginning teachers develop guidelines and criteria for making decisions in the classroom and in other aspects of their work. More experienced teachers may find the book helpful as a springboard for reflection and discussion among themselves or as a stimulus to writing cases of their own.

The book has been designed for use in methods courses and workshops and by teachers who pursue professional development on their own. It not intended to take the place of a comprehensive textbook but should be used as a supplement to other teaching materials in an elementary science methods course. Instructors of methods courses should note, however, that examples of inquiry-based teaching included in some of the cases can serve to reinforce other aspects of the pre-service curriculum.

The first chapter introduces the reader to the use of case studies in teaching and explains why case studies are particularly appropriate in science teacher education. Chapters 2 through 5 comprise case studies categorized by the type of problem addressed. Chapter 2 focuses on problems encountered and decisions made in student teaching; chapter 3 focuses on classroom management. Chapter 4 contains cases that arose during inquiry-based classroom instruction, and chapter 5 looks at some difficulties encountered in maintaining constructive relations with colleagues, administrators, and parents.

We have identified sixteen types of problems or areas of concern that are addressed in some way in these cases. Some are the primary focus of the case study; others are secondary but nevertheless required the teacher to make a decision. These have been classified under four broad topics: Instruction, Human Relations, Cultural Awareness, and Ethical Dilemmas. The chart that follows the preface indicates the types of problems that are addressed in each of the cases and provides a quick reference for students or instructors who wish to find a case to meet a particular instructional emphasis or other professional need.

The final chapter takes the reader beyond the case studies in the book, offering a persuasive argument for teachers to write and study their own accounts of incidents and decisions as a means of growing and learning from their experience as teachers.

Teachers have shared their stories in the hope that what they have learned can be passed on to other teachers and future teachers who want to include science as a vital, exciting part of the curriculum. We hope that the study of these cases will stimulate reflection and discussion and help teachers make thoughtful decisions to support science teaching in the elementary school.

◼ Acknowledgments

The teachers and future teachers who shared their experiences with us made this book possible. They brought to the task a wide range of ages, years of teaching, and perspectives on teaching. The fact that almost all are women reflects the composition of teaching staffs in the schools of the mid-South and Southwest where these teachers live and work. That the majority are Euro-American with a minority of African-Americans and Hispanics also reflects the composition of teaching staffs in the schools of these regions.

No real names are used in the text; we have changed all teachers' names as well as the names of the schools where they teach. The following are the real names of the teachers whom we acknowledge and thank for their time, their interest in this project, and their contributions to the education of the next generation of teachers: Julia Beamon, Glenda Bell, Chris Brandt, Nancy Bray, Mary Callery, Glenda Carter, Kathy Donk, Allison Hailey, Ann Hancock, Leigh Ann Janney, Duranda Keen, Jennifer Kennedy, Terrie Kielborn, Priscilla Person, Sylvia Shepherd, Betsy Sullivan, Pat Thornton, Cindy Vainwright, Shelly Watson, and Jill White. We also acknowledge with thanks the contributions of Dr. Cheryl Grable and her students: Ron Atkinson, Verdell Bunting, Erica Craft, and Angela Sparrow.

We extend special thanks to all those at Prentice Hall who have guided and supported us: to Bradley Potthoff for his advice and patience, to Mary Evangelista for answering endless questions, and to Jennifer Day who took Mary's place at a crucial moment. We thank the reviewers of our manuscript for their insights and comments: Richard L. Benoit, University of Houston—Clear Lake; Thomas Giles, Cumberland College; Cheryl Grable, University of Arkansas at Little Rock; Michael Kamen, Auburn University; Rita K. Voltmer, Miami University; Edward J. Zielinski, Clarion University; and Douglas P. Zook, Boston University

We also acknowledge and thank our husbands, Charles Howe and Tony Thompson, who support and encourage us in all our professional endeavors, including this one.

CASES

Groupings: **Instruction** (Planning, Obtaining Resources, Capturing Student Interest, Strategies for Inquiry, Modeling/Designing, Developmentally Appropriate, Using Technology, Assessment) · **Human Relations** (Teacher-Disruptive Student, Teacher-Prospective Teacher, Teacher-Parent, Teacher-Teacher, Teacher-Administrator) · **Cultural Awareness** (Professional Culture, Classroom Culture, Home Culture, Including All Students) · **Ethical Dilemmas**

No.	Title	Level	Content	Planning	Obtaining Resources	Capturing Student Interest	Strategies for Inquiry	Modeling/Designing	Developmentally Appropriate	Using Technology	Assessment	Teacher-Disruptive Student	Teacher-Prospective Teacher	Teacher-Parent	Teacher-Teacher	Teacher-Administrator	Professional Culture	Classroom Culture	Home Culture	Including All Students	Ethical Dilemmas
2.1	Kaboom, Kaput	P	Phys	●		●	●														
2.2	The Model Science Lesson	P	Life/Phys					●									●				
2.3	Having Great and Not So Great Expectations	P	ES										●								
2.4	But We've Always Done It this Way	UE	—										●								
2.5	Weathering The Storm	P	ES			●		●		●										●	
2.6	Surfing into a Science Research Quandary	UE	—							●				●				●			
3.1	I Won't Sit with Girls	P	—									●						●			
3.2	Accentuate the Positive	UE	—									●							●		
3.3	No, I Won't!	UE	Life			●						●									
3.4	Carpet Capers	P	Phys				●								●						●
3.5	Help! How Can I Teach Without Supplies	—	—		●																
4.1	Spider!	P	Life	●		●	●	●													
4.2	Make Way for Tadpoles	P	Life			●	●				●										
4.3	Building Castles	UE	Phys			●	●	●												●	
4.4	Don't Sink the Concept	UE	Phys	●		●	●	●													
4.5	Hands of Surgeons, Minds of Scientists	P	Life			●	●														
4.6	Haz Tu Tarea (Do Your School Work)	UE	ES													●				●	
4.7	What's Wrong with Them?	P	—																		
4.8	On Rembrandts, Shakespeares, and Copycats	P	Phys			●	●	●			●										●
4.9	Warming Up to Animals	P	Life						●												
4.10	We Lost the Science Fair	P	Life						●		●							●			
5.1	Barbara's Mother	P	Life						●					●							
5.2	Tommy's Father	UE	—											●							
5.3	Father Knows Best	UE	—				●	●			●			●					●		●
5.4	Whose Bird Nest?	UE	Life											●							
5.5	First-Year Teacher	P	—												●	●	●				
5.6	Setting Children Up for Failure	UE	—								●					●	●				●
5.7	Science Partners and Uncertain Liaisons	UE	Phys							●								●			

P = Primary, Grades K–3; UE = Upper Elementary, Grades 4–6; Phys = Physical Science; Life = Life Science; ES = Earth Science

vi

Contents

1

Cases as Guides to Learning to Teach Science

Learning to teach science is very different from learning about science. Each science discipline has a definite structure; there are theories and laws that apply regardless of conditions as well as rules or procedures for solving problems. In contrast, science teaching has no laws that apply regardless of context and no rules for solving problems that arise in the classroom. Successful science teachers must first gain command of their subject matter; but beyond that, most of the knowledge of teaching has to be created in interaction with instructors, mentors, peers and, finally, students themselves.

There is no one right way to teach anything, including science. Children have different ways of learning and teachers develop different teaching styles, depending on the children they teach and their own personalities. The cases in this book will give you glimpses of how some teachers teach science and how they have dealt with problems in the classroom as well as those involving parents, colleagues, and administrators. Becoming a competent, effective teacher is not something that can be taught; learning to teach is a process that can be guided by instructors and mentors and stimulated by interaction with peers, but in the final analysis, what kind of teacher you become will depend on your own motivation and effort.

Constructivism in Teacher Education

The main idea of constructivism is that knowledge is not transmitted directly from one person to another but is actively constructed by the learner. A great deal has been written about children's misconceptions concerning scientific phenomena and what may be done to promote development of scientific concepts (Driver, Asoko, Leach, Mortimer and Scott, 1994; Solomon, 1994). Constructivist ideas can also be applied to learning to teach science. Fosnot (1989), a thoughtful teacher educator who uses constructivist ideas in her work with teachers, has outlined four principles of constructivism (pp. 19–20). These are listed below with our own interpretations and elaborations.

1. New knowledge is built on past constructions.

Knowledge that has been constructed by the learner is the basis on which new knowledge is built. This refers to new knowledge that is internalized and permanent, not to facts that can be memorized and subsequently forgotten.

2. Constructions come about through assimilation and accommodation.

Knowledge is built by assimilating new ideas or experiences and accommodating, or modifying, old knowledge to include the new. For example, you may think that all third grade classes in the same school will be very similar and that you will be able to use the same teaching materials, with small changes, from one year to the next. That is a past construction of knowledge that seems reasonable. However, one of the cases in this book describes a third grade class that was very different from the previous year's class. The teacher was presented with something new and unexpected and had to change her old conception to assimilate, or accept, this new knowledge and make room for it; that is, accommodate it, in a new understanding of children. This is a simple example of assimilation and accommodation to construct new knowledge.

3.   Learning is a process of invention rather than accumulation.

Fosnot uses the term *invention* to denote creating something that is new to the learner. Knowledge that is useful in our lives is not built up by memorizing facts and adding them all together, but by thinking about the facts, ideas, and experiences we have and connecting them to each other and to those things we already know.

4.   Meaningful learning occurs through reflection and resolution of cognitive conflict.

Meaningful learning is learning that has meaning in our lives and, like other things that have meaning to us, is not arrived at easily or quickly. None of us likes to give up cherished ideas. Cognitive conflict is the term used to describe the experience of confronting new knowledge that conflicts with what we already know or thought we knew. Constructivist theory focuses on the mental activity of individuals as they wrestle with assimilation of new ideas and try to resolve the cognitive conflict caused by the need to fit the new ideas into an already existing system of concepts.

The process of knowledge construction is sometimes represented by a series of concept maps. A concept map is a diagram that represents a person's understanding of how ideas or concepts related to a topic are connected and interconnected (Novak, 1990; Wandersee, 1990). An example is shown in Figure 1.1. This map shows how concept maps are tied to curriculum development and are linked to other related concepts.

Suppose you made a concept map of what you now know or believe about teaching elementary science, linking all concepts related to that topic in ways that represent your understanding of the connections between them. Then, after studying the cases in this book, suppose you had formed new concepts, made changes in existing concepts and seen new relationships and were asked to construct another concept map. You would have to decide how to fit the new or altered concepts into the old map and revise it to represent your changed understandings. Notice that although the concept map would be revised, it would not be thrown away because new knowledge is built on what is already known. The revised concept map would represent the new knowledge that you had constructed. Beyerbach and Smith (1990) showed that this is what happened when they used concept maps to study preservice teachers' evolving constructions of the concept *effective teaching*.

The idea that teachers must construct their own concepts about teaching is supported by the National Science Education Standards (NSES) published in 1996 by

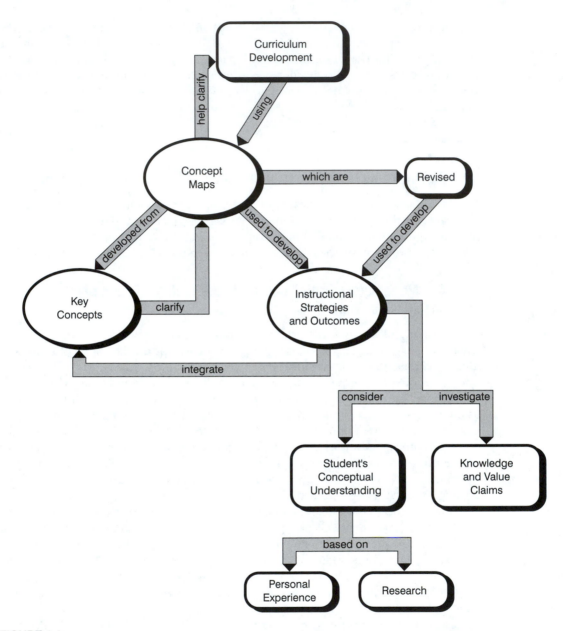

FIGURE 1.1

Concept Map of Curriculum Development

From "Heuristic for Curriculum Development" by M. Starr and J. Krajcik, 1990, *Journal of Research in Science Teaching*, 27(10), p. 990. Copyright 1990 by John Wiley & Sons. Adapted by permission.

the National Research Council. NSES is a series of recommendations involving all aspects of science education, including the professional development of preservice teachers as well as those now in practice. One of the recommendations is a change in emphasis from "teacher as consumer about knowledge of teaching" to "teacher as producer of knowledge about teaching" (p. 72).

Two Ways of Knowing: Propositional and Narrative

If constructivism focuses on the mental activity of individuals as they wrestle with assimilation of new ideas, it is logical to ask, "Where do the ideas come from?" For almost a century education has been influenced by a psychology of learning that assumed that there was a body of knowledge, separate from the learner, to be memorized, comprehended, and applied. This is referred to as scientific or propositional knowledge and is one way of knowing about and understanding what goes on around us. Scientific knowledge is based on propositions that are general and impersonal and that are learned as concepts, theories or principles. Some of these are referred to as laws of nature. One of these laws is that water runs downhill everywhere on earth. Others are that the movements of the sun and moon are known and predictable and that the acceleration of a body of given mass in a known gravitational field can be represented by a specific formula. The main question asked about this kind of knowledge is, "Under what conditions is this valid?" The more general the knowledge is, the more highly it is regarded.

Much of what we learn in school is this kind of knowledge, including theories not only in the field of science but also in the fields of psychology, economics, sociology, and education. A central task of the school, at every level, is to teach this body of knowledge with the expectation that students will store it in memory; if they question the validity of the knowledge, the questions are properly raised on logical or rational grounds. Students work to understand the concepts and learn the rules, formulas, and circumstances under which the rules apply. Teachers work to motivate and engage their students in learning things often removed from the students' experience. And we have all noticed that unless we have reason to apply the theories to specific instances or use the knowledge in some way in our lives, the concepts and rules and theories tend to fade away and gradually become more difficult to recall.

Scientific knowledge is an important way of knowing about the world, but it is not the only way. Another means is through stories or narratives that are personal rather than impersonal, closer to our daily lives and understood through feeling and emotion rather than logic and reason. They are specific to a time and place and are remembered without having to be memorized; they can foster understanding in ways that cannot be achieved by expositions of facts, principles and theories. Learning from stories is a very old and powerful way of learning that can complement other ways of learning and knowing. We hear a story and, if it rings true, it lodges in our memory without any conscious effort. Think of the stories told in your family; although some are new, others have been handed down from generation to generation and you will retell them yourself to the next generation. Although most of you have probably forgotten many of the *dates* in American history, you remember the stories of the first settlers and the pioneers who opened the West. The stories are about real people and we can relate to them.

Science teaching can be guided, to some extent, by scientific theories derived from psychology, sociology, and other disciplines. As examples, behaviorist theories are the basis for many systems of classroom management, cognitive developmental theories are the basis for much of the curriculum development in science, and sociocultural theories have recently gained acceptance as the basis for some kinds of classroom organization. Although we do not deny the importance of theoretical knowledge, we believe that this knowledge will be more meaningful to you after you have had classroom experience and can place your experience within a theoretical perspective. The teachers' stories in this book may convey more powerful meaning than theoretical knowledge as you begin to learn to practice a profession that is complex and unpredictable and sometimes seems to be both unscientific and illogical.

Case Studies as Guides to Practice

The limits of theory as a guide to instructional practice have been recognized by some educational psychologists and theorists themselves. Korthagen and Kessels (1999), in discussing the difference between reasoning based on general principles and the concerns of instructional practice, argue that practical classroom problems do not always have fixed solutions that can be found by applying a particular scientific theory. Research on teaching and learning is increasingly moving out of the laboratory and into the classroom. This trend is evident in the field of mathematics as explained and illustrated by mathematics educators Cobb and Bowers (1999) but is also occurring in science education. For example, Shulman (1992) had this to say about using cases as guides to practice rather than applications of theory:

> Practical decisions are not deducible from general principles. Theoretical principles play a key role in practical arguments, but they share that role with the distinctive features and broad categories of past cases and the particular textual details of present circumstances. (p. 16)

Teaching is a very practical endeavor with many of the characteristics of a craft. The practice of a craft requires skill and thought and, in the hands of a master, is raised to the level of art. Traditionally, and still today, a craft is learned through apprenticeship to a master craftsperson. The novice learns by watching and working side by side with the master. This is the same function that case studies can have; the prospective teacher or beginning teacher learns from reading and thinking about and then discussing the thoughts and actions of the expert teacher. That analogy is only partially applicable here because we have included some cases from the experiences of beginning teachers as well as those from experienced teachers. The essential point is that teaching is undergirded more by practical knowledge based on experience than by knowledge of theoretical constructs.

■ Case Studies as Carriers of Values

A case study begins with a teacher's account of a real incident or situation that required a decision. The case studies presented here recount a particular incident from a science class or a situation that arose from interpersonal interactions associated in some way with teaching science. Entering into the experience of the narrator, the reader's own thoughts and feelings are evoked to make the case meaningful and memorable. As the reader becomes involved in the story and understands the problem from the teacher's point of view, the values that underlie the decision become more apparent and help the reader to clarify his or her own values. Questions of fairness, honesty, and ethical behavior in responding to the demands of teaching science may be implicit or explicit but they are seldom absent in these cases.

We have explained that cases in this book are used primarily as a guide to the practice of teaching science rather than as examples of teachers applying theory to practice. Not all undergraduates have a firm grasp of the various theories that they have studied, but by the end of their undergraduate education, students have developed their own ethical and moral values; the application of values to decision making in science teaching happens whether we intend it or not.

Sometimes the values seem clear when a teacher takes a moment to reflect. An example is the decision that one of the teachers makes as she decides to abandon her science lesson plan when the children discover a spider and want to learn more about it. The teacher decides that allowing children to pursue their interest and curiosity at that moment is more important than the lesson planned. This is a "teachable moment" that will be lost if postponed.

In other cases the values are not so clearly defined or the best course to follow is not apparent because there are conflicting values. In one case study involving experiments related to the story of Archimedes and the Golden Crown, the teacher asks whether it is better for the children to pursue their own questions, which she knows will lead to a dead end, or to focus on the activity designed to help them learn an important science concept. Here there are two important values in conflict with each other: one is letting children pursue their own ideas and the other is directing them toward learning an important concept. While neither choice is completely satisfactory, the teacher must choose between the two.

Learning to make decisions and to live with them is part of becoming a teacher. Often you will have to make a decision when quick action is called for and there is no time to think it through. You take the risk of making a wrong decision because you cannot do nothing; you must act and do the best you can. At other times a problem remains unresolved and you will have plenty of time but no obvious basis for making a decision. All possible courses of action seem to have the potential for undesirable consequences. In spite of this, you have to address the problem or become disengaged in the lives of the children, and risk becoming the kind of teacher who turns children off.

Decision making is never completely guided by reason or conscious thought; each decision is influenced in ways that we may or may not be aware of at the time. One of the purposes of this book is to help you increase your awareness of what is happening around you and to raise to consciousness some of the unconscious feelings and memories that influence your own decision making. These are matters of perception rather than cognition. Some of the factors are feelings about students and about yourself, former experiences and your own values. Your understanding of your role as a teacher plays a part, whether you think of yourself as responsible for giving correct answers or instead for helping your students find answers themselves. Studying cases of the dilemmas faced and the decisions made by other teachers can be a means of bringing your own values into clearer focus and will lead to making conscious value-based decisions when the occasion demands it.

■ Four Perspectives for Looking at Cases

In this section we describe four perspectives from which to view the problems presented in these cases as well as problems you will encounter when you are teaching. These perspectives, or lenses, have been used for looking at business organizations (McNeill-Miller, 1999) but would seem to be useful in educational situations as well. In suggesting these four perspectives, we do not intend to imply that there is only one perspective from which to look at a case; it may be helpful to try several perspectives in considering a case and decide which is more useful in finding possible solutions or a resolution. Each of the four perspectives leads to questions to ask yourself or, possibly, to discuss with your classmates.

Structural Perspective.   Is the problem one of structure, either in the classroom, the school or the community? Is the structure the teacher has set up in the classroom appropriate to the goals? Could the problem be solved by a change in rules or the exercise of more or less authority?

Sometimes an inappropriate structure can be changed by the teacher. For example, at the beginning of the school year the teacher establishes rules and guidelines for children's behavior in the classroom, on field trips, at a Science Fair and for any other activities where the teacher is responsible for the children's conduct and safety. When the teacher finds that the structure that has been established is not working, he or she can change the rules or practices. This may involve a change in students' seating arrangements, allowing more time in science class for cleaning up, or establishing clearer guidelines for assigning responsibility for classroom tasks.

On the other hand, when parents, administrators, or people in the community are involved, it is often more difficult to change the structure. One case presents the problem of community people who want to be involved in teaching science but obviously need clear guidelines for working with children.

Human Relations Perspective.   Are there important needs of students that are not being met? Are the energy and talents of students being used? Is the problem one of the teacher or other participant not being sensitive to the human relations aspects of the situation?

Beginning teachers can become so involved in planning interesting lessons, maintaining a task-oriented atmosphere in the classroom, and meeting all the demands of the system that they may not be able to focus on the needs of individual children or on the group dynamics within the classroom. Since children's lives are to a large extent focused on school, it is important for school to be a positive experience for them. Relations with other adults are also important. Conscientious parents are rightly concerned about their children's educations and they need to know that the teacher is doing all that is possible to promote learning and growth.

Political Perspective. Many important decisions involve the allocation of resources and are resolved through negotiation and bargaining. Individuals and groups differ in their beliefs, values, preferences and perceptions of reality. Has the teacher recognized the legitimate interests and different perspectives of the groups or individuals she or he is working with? Can there be some kind of compromise or negotiation?

Politics is used here in a broad sense, referring to the competition between groups for resources, power, and leadership, what is sometimes referred to as a "power struggle." One of the difficult things about teaching is that a teacher has to deal with so many individuals and groups, each of which may have different interests.

Parents who want their children to do well in school sometimes think that the teacher is giving lower grades than deserved. Although parents have a legitimate interest in wanting their children to succeed, the teacher has to assign grades based on standards that have been set. Another example is a conflict than can arise between an experienced teacher and a preservice teacher who has been assigned to his or her class. The preservice teacher is eager to try out things learned in methods class; the experienced teacher wants to ensure that all class time is put to best use for the children's benefit.

Symbolic Perspective. It is not always possible to know exactly what happened at any one time during a busy and often confusing day, but individuals often interpret events symbolically. How have those involved interpreted the meaning of what happened? Did it mean the same thing to all those involved? Did an incident have a symbolic meaning to a child or colleague that is not understood by the teacher? Did it trigger a memory of a painful or happy experience?

As an example of a problem that has a symbolic component, take the issue of students wearing hats in classrooms. No one can seriously think that a small inconspicuous hat prevents the wearer from learning or that the hat itself would prevent other students from learning. However, removing one's hat is a sign of respect and to refuse to do so is taken as a symbol of defiance by those in authority, although the student simply may see it as a way to express individuality. The problem of hat wearing could be considered from all of the four perspectives but the symbolic perspective cannot be ignored. When a student wears hats to class, he or she is using them as a symbol to say something to the world.

■ Special Challenges in Teaching Science

An effective science program involves children in activities that require special equipment and apparatus and allows children some degree of freedom to move about the classroom as they carry out their work. This kind of program presents challenges in classroom management that are not presented by other, less activity-centered programs where the children are not handling equipment or animals, do not do field work outside the classroom and do not need as much opportunity to move about while completing their tasks.

Some special materials and pieces of equipment are very attractive to children and stimulate some children to become excited and to go beyond acceptable limits of behavior. Children who have always had to be quiet and keep to their seats in school have to learn a new set of behaviors for science class where they are free to move about, talk quietly to neighbors and handle interesting objects. It is the teacher's responsibility to guide the children in learning what behavior is acceptable and what is unacceptable in science class.

We know that children should be encouraged and given opportunities to learn from each other as well as from the teacher. Coaching children as they learn appropriate behaviors for science class and organizing the classroom to facilitate the kind of interactions that promote student-to-student learning will allow you to concentrate your attention on guiding children toward construction of new knowledge.

Another kind of challenge in science teaching is presented by the need to take into account children's ideas and preconceptions about many of the scientific phenomena that form the content basis of the curriculum. Take, for example, children's ideas about the shape of the earth. Their experience tells them that the earth is flat except for mountains here and there over the surface. There is nothing in their experience that leads them to believe otherwise and they will not change this deeply held conviction as the result of hearing from the teacher that the earth is round. They have to have time to think about it, to turn it over in their minds.

Not all of the misconceptions or alternative conceptions that children have are the product of their own minds acting freely on their experiences; some come from things they have been told or taught in ways that lead to erroneous assumptions and conclusions. A child who believes, in the deepest way, that the earth is flat will reconcile the idea that the earth is "round" by thinking of the earth as a flat, round disk and will say, when asked, that she knows that the earth is round. The teacher assumes she is thinking of a ball but the child is thinking of a pancake. Teaching without models has led the child to form this misconception. Concepts that are counterintuitive or that are based on abstract ideas or things too large or too small to be seen directly are a special challenge in science teaching.

To get around this problem, teachers often use analogies to explain abstract concepts but this, too, can lead to misunderstanding, particularly when an analogy is taken too literally. For example, the flow of electricity through a wire is sometimes taught as analogous to water flowing through a pipe. Children, not unreasonably, assume that electricity is a substance, like water.

Much of what we know about how children learn science has come from the study of how individual children perform tasks or solve problems in isolation. Intelligence tests consist of a series of problems to be solved, whether by a preschooler matching shapes or a high school senior puzzling out the meaning of a passage of text, always by an individual on his or her own. The study of how children learn school subjects, including science, is based on experiments that follow roughly the same pattern. But you will not be teaching one on one; you will be teaching a group of children, and psychology has much less to say about that.

The case studies in this book address these and other challenges in science teaching. They challenge *you* to be open to broadening your knowledge and understanding of what it means to be a science teacher.

■ Summary

In this chapter we have presented a constructivist view of learning to teach science and described two kinds of knowledge, propositional and narrative. The main purpose of studying cases, which are themselves narratives, is to gain insight into the practical, rather than the theoretical, aspects of teaching science. Another purpose is to become aware of the way a teacher's values are expressed in the decisions that are made and to become more aware of the values that are important to you. We presented four perspectives or frameworks for looking at cases; these will be referred to in later chapters as we suggest ideas for reflection and discussion. In the final section of the chapter you are reminded of some of the special challenges of teaching science to children.

> The bad news is that there are no simple answers to "What do you do when . . . " questions that come out of the classroom. . . . Therefore, the best that teachers can hope for are the tools that allow them to perceive dilemmas with intelligence and sensitivity and to make thoughtful, informed decisions that guide teaching action. (Wasserman, 1993, pp. 6, 8).

Questions for Discussion and Reflection

1. Give examples from your experience of problems or issues that were mainly (a) structural, (b) involving human relations, (c) political, and (d) symbolic.

2. Draw a concept map of your overall concept of yourself as a science teacher.

3. Give an example from your own life of learning something important from a story or narrative. Choose something that you could not or would not have known if you had not heard or read the story.

4. Describe an incident or event from your own school days that made a lasting impression on you. Members of a group can share their stories.

5. Do you feel more excited or more apprehensive about teaching science? Discuss this with a classmate or group to share your feelings.

2

Prospective Teachers
Making Classroom Decisions

Cases in this chapter address issues associated with introducing prospective teachers to science teaching through their participation in teachers' classrooms. Some of the cases are written from the future teacher's point of view; others are written from the supervising teacher's perspective.

Making the transition from student to teacher is a challenging time in the journey towards becoming a professional educator. If you are a prospective teacher, you already have spent fourteen or more years as a student and have observed the practices of many teachers. Your ideas about what science is and how to teach it necessarily reflect your prior experiences in learning science. You have probably developed criteria, consciously or unconsciously, about what makes a good science teacher. Now it's time to shift your focus from being a student to being a teacher. That's not always easy because it's one thing to have experiences as a student and to have opinions about teaching, but it's another matter to understand the ideas and decisions that inform teachers' practices.

Substantive experiences with teachers and students in classrooms should be a part of preparing to become a teacher. Ideally, these experiences will take place with teachers who not only model the best science teaching practices, but also take time to mentor a student through reflective practice. Experiences in the classroom will expose you to learning about children whose experiences are vastly different from your own. And, under the best circumstances, you will have opportunities to learn about creating professional communities that can continue to support your learning about teaching. However, as in other areas of life, the ideal in field-based learning is not always attained, either for the prospective teacher or for the supervising teacher.

In this book, cases written by classroom teachers reflect some of the tensions created by their attempts to facilitate the learning of prospective teachers without neglecting the learning of their own elementary students. Prospective teachers have contributed cases that describe their experiences learning among other prospective teachers, classroom teachers, and students. As you read, you will begin to sense the complex nature of decision making unique to teacher preparation. At times, you will feel the tensions experienced by prospective teachers as they strive to meet the expectations of university instructors, classroom teachers, and elementary students. Likewise, classroom teachers may be placed in awkward positions when there are limited opportunities to negotiate and clarify the roles of persons coming into their classrooms to perform teaching activities. Through your study of these cases, you may identify situations that encourage problems to take place, and be aware of important decisions that could have been made in advance to avoid such dilemmas. Other cases will introduce you to some of the feelings teachers experience as they encounter new and unexpected situations, and learn the art of making uncertain decisions.

■ ■ ■

Kaboom, Kaput!

This case, written by a prospective elementary teacher named Ella, is about an experience she had during a field-based teaching activity. The classroom teacher had worked
with the university science methods instructor to design this science field experience for
prospective teachers enrolled in the course. The assignment involved prospective elementary teachers sharing a science experiment with groups of children in the teacher's
classroom. The experiment intrigued the children; however, Ella was confused when she
found it difficult to facilitate discussion with children following the experiment.

We weren't sure what to expect when our science methods instructor, Dr.
Olsen, told us we were going to observe an "eggs-citing egg-speriment." Dr.
Olsen peeled the shell off a hard-boiled egg, then asked several participants
to make observations of the egg. The observations were listed on the board and
included descriptions such as color, texture, and estimated weight of the boiled egg.
She then showed us a glass bottle that was similarly observed; we decided it was an
apple cider jar based on its unique shape. We watched closely as she placed the jar
on the counter, lit a stick of newspaper, and dropped it into the jar. The egg was
immediately placed over the opening of the jar. I saw the egg make a few "hops" as a
slight wisp of smoke escaped out of the bottle. The jar filled with smoke, and the fire
stick went out. Immediately, the egg made a "Kaboom" sound as it popped into the
bottle! We all gasped in surprise! Dr. Olsen asked us to write a description of what
we had seen and an explanation for what happened in our journals. I wrote:

> I saw the egg sucked into the bottle with a lot of force. I know that the bottle didn't
> actually "suck" the egg inside, but I'm not sure how else to describe what happened! I
> suspect that the fire used up all the oxygen, thus creating a vacuum inside the jar. The
> egg got sucked in because of the vacuum. I have to admit that, as I'm thinking this
> through, I am wondering, "What is a 'vacuum' really?" I've heard, and used, this word in

science, but I can't seem to use it now to explain what I saw happen. I loved this experiment, though—it was a great trick!

We spent some time sharing our journal entries in large group discussion. Dr. Olsen had drawn two columns on a large sheet of paper and recorded, as we talked, our observations and explanations. I noticed that several others had, like me, bumped into the word vacuum, but didn't really understand how it worked in this experiment. Dr. Olsen created a third column to record our "problem words." At first, it was fun listening to everyone's ideas, but after 20 minutes we were ready to hear the "official" explanation from Dr. Olsen. A classmate asked, "So what's the real explanation for why this happened?" Dr. Olsen responded by saying that she wanted us to imagine we were a group of scientists and this was the first time we had conducted this experiment. No answer could be given to us—we would have to decide as a group which of our explanations seemed most acceptable based on our observations. I'm not sure we ever really understood the concept of "vacuum," but the class voted the "vacuum" explanation to be the most acceptable explanation for the experiment.

Dr. Olsen redirected our attention to focus on a new assignment; we were going to conduct this experiment in a K–1 classroom for our next class session! It was one thing for us to play around with this experiment with my adult classmates, but the thought of doing this experiment with a group of children was a bit unnerving! What if it didn't work right? How would I explain to the kids what happened to the egg? I had an entire weekend to be both excited and worried about conducting the experiment. I actually had a nightmare in which everyone was looking at me, and I was supposed to explain the experiment, but no words would come out of my mouth! While I looked forward to teaching science to real children, I was somewhat dreading the unexpected!

Tuesday morning arrived. We found ourselves looking at a very excited group of 18 children in Ms. Kessell's K–1 classroom. We had planned in advance to break up into four small groups and have one adult in each group serve as the facilitator— the person to actually lead the activity. Others from our group were to take note of the children's responses, to help as needed with materials for the experiment, and to serve as safety monitors. (Dr. Olsen had provided goggles for all of us to wear as a way to model safe science. The kids loved seeing the garb of real scientists!)

For some reason, what happened next set into motion a sequence of events that turned my nightmare into a reality! One group had quickly gotten the experiment underway, and, before anyone expected it, we heard "Kaboom!" Everyone froze and looked in the direction of the sound. Students in this first group stood with their mouths open, and eyes big as saucers. Excited laughter and voices began to erupt around the room: "Wow!" "Did you see that?" "What happened?" A boy in group one announced, "Hey, look, that group's egg is about to go!" The first group quickly moved over to join the group at the second table who had just placed their fire stick into their bottle. (My group and another group ceased doing our own work and looked to see what was going on in group two.) "Kaboom!" A second egg was sucked into a bottle! The combined groups of 1 and 2 now looked excitedly at a third group who had not yet conducted the experiment. A mass of bodies poured over to the table of the third group to see if their egg would have the same fate. Then, "Kaboom!" Voila—what fun!

I stood mesmerized. It had all happened so quickly! I stood holding the fire stick in one hand and boiled egg in the other. Suddenly, my legs became noodles as I saw the entire classroom join my table group. I was terrified! I took a deep breath, smiled, and tried to focus on the activity. Everyone in the classroom was now gathered around our table.

I asked for quiet, then passed around the egg for children in our group to observe. As I'd seen Dr. Olsen do in class, I asked for observations about the egg and bottle. I wanted them to see that these were ordinary materials—that this was not a magic trick of some sort. My hands trembled as I lit the fire stick and dropped it into the bottle. In a flash, I placed the egg on top of the bottle. I panicked—the egg didn't move! I was about to remove the egg to redo the experiment, when someone from our adult group pointed out, "Look, it's moving—but verrry slowly!" It *was* moving, and moments later we heard "Kaboom!" I could hear a small voice in my head saying, "Whew—it worked!"

My moment of relief was short-lived. Everyone was now looking at me. I began asking the children to share their observations. I tried to get their attention so I could teach them about the point of the experiment—that air can push things into places where there is less air. I tried to facilitate the discussion, but disorder began to surface among the students. Those standing farther away from the table quickly lost interest and began wandering away from the table area. Others struggled to have more space around them, nudging and shoving their neighbors. Goggles became interesting play masks. Those nearest the table wanted to explore materials used in the experiment. I could see tiny hands and fingers reaching out from all sides. What was I supposed to do now? Everything was getting out of control. Forget about bringing closure to the activity—everything had gone kaput!

Pause for Reflection:

What would you do at this point if you were the student teacher in this case?

What seemed like quite a long time was actually seconds before Ms. Kessell intervened. She stepped up from the rear of the room to the tableside, asked everyone to gather around the table, and resumed the discussion by asking the children, "What are some questions you have? Let's hear just a few." One child raised her hand and asked, "Why did the egg go into the bottle?" Ms. Kessell acknowledged the question, "Good question! Does someone else have a question?" The group regained focus as more questions were offered by the students, "Would the egg get pulled in faster if we made a bigger fire in the jar?" "Can you get the egg back out?" Ms. Kessell thanked the students for their interesting questions, and then called attention to one boy's question, "Let's take a minute to explore one question: Why did the fire go out?" She started the exploration by asking the group, "What are some things you know about fire?" Several responses were heard: "Fires need air." "Fire burns paper." "Fires use oxygen." "Fires need water." Ms. Kessell was surprised at the last response. "Fires need water. Would you please share with us why you think fires need water?" she asked the student. The boy responded, "Because I've always heard that you should have water with fires." Ms. Kessell asked the group, "Do fires need water?"

Some heads nodded yes, while others shook no. "Let's put that question to the test. Let's do an experiment."

Ms. Kessell sent a student to the classroom sink to get a glass of water. While waiting for the student to return, Ms. Kessell reminded the group that they would have to continue practicing "safe science" during the experiment. She asked the students to review what this meant—keeping their hands by their sides, standing calmly next to their neighbors. She indicated that she would continue wearing her goggles, but it would be safe for everyone else to pass their goggles to the university teachers. With the glass of water now placed on the table, Ms. Kessell proceeded with the experiment. She restated the original question for the group: "The question we are exploring is, 'Do fires need water?'" She told the children she would light a paper fire stick and then put it in the water to see what would happen. Before she proceeded further, she asked the children to predict what would happen. Several children raised their hands and, when called upon, predicted that the fire would go out. A class vote was taken to see how many others agreed or disagreed with the prediction. The fire stick was lit and quickly dunked into the glass of water. They were right—the fire went out! She asked the students to share what they observed about putting fire and water together. Comments included, "Water drowns fire," "Fire can't burn water." The group seemed satisfied and ready to explore new questions. A student asked, "So what is the black stuff on the glass?" Ms. Kessell rubbed her finger in the "black stuff" inside the neck of the jar used in the egg experiment. She held up her finger and said. "That *is* an interesting question, Why do fires leave black stuff behind? I think we'll save that question to explore during science time tomorrow."

Ms. Kessell noted the time and asked the children to quickly get ready for lunch—they were running late. She had the children say "Thanks" to the university visitors. We returned a "Thank you" and waved good-bye as the children marched out the door. I wondered to myself, "What would happen during science time tomorrow if I were the teacher of Ms. Kessell's classroom? Would we pursue an experiment to learn about the 'black stuff'?"

Analysis and Discussion

1. If you are a student teacher, or remember when you were one, what feelings does this story evoke?

2. What do you think would have happened next if Ms. Kessell had not stepped in? If you were in Ella's place, would you rather have Ms. Kessell step in or leave it to you to handle the situation?

3. Were you content with the "vacuum" explanation offered by the writer of this case? What explanation would you offer to another adult to explain why the egg goes into the bottle?

4. Ms. Kessell decided to follow up the initial experiment by exploring questions generated by the children. Do you think these questions are relevant toward understanding why the egg is drawn into the bottle?

5. Experiments such as this are often referred to in tradebooks as "science tricks to amaze friends." Why might an experiment like this one be perceived as a magic trick? What problems might develop if students perceive science activities as magic tricks? What can a teacher do to change a magic trick into a scientific understanding?

6. Based on content recommendations for grades K–4 in the National Science Education Standards, what science themes and concepts could be addressed through the egg and bottle experiment? Draw a concept map to show related science themes and concepts.

■ ■ ■

Case 2.2   The Model Science Lesson

This case was written by Doloris, an undergraduate completing her final year of study in a university elementary–middle grades teacher education program. Doloris is an advocate of using multiple approaches to engage students in science learning. In this case, she highlights the use of such visual aids as drawings and science demonstration, while teaching a lesson in a science methods class and also while teaching a unit about weather in a local second grade elementary classroom. Both situations pose problems related to Doloris's use of models, and her experience provides us with an opportunity to consider the role of models in science learning and teaching.

My hands and voice shook as I began to teach my 5–E (Engage, Explore, Explain, Elaborate, Evaluate) lesson plan to the other students in my science methods class. This was my first teacher education class at the university, and, since it was science, I was on unfamiliar ground any way I looked at it! My lesson was actually part of a plant unit I had designed for a class assignment.

I began by reading a children's book: *Tops and Bottoms* by Janet Stevens. My voice quivered and my hands shook as I held the book up for everyone to see. The class seemed to enjoy the story and I soon began to feel and sound less nervous. I followed the story with a brief discussion, and highlighted the idea that you *can* tell a plant by its seed cover.

Then, I introduced a hands-on activity to examine seeds. I organized the class into small groups and gave each a little white tray containing various seeds. I instructed the group, "Please look through the seeds on your tray. You might like to use your hand lenses to help you make better observations. I want you to predict what sorts of plants you think will come from these seeds." On the chalkboard, I had listed the various types of seeds I had included on their trays. The class spent a few minutes looking at the seeds and guessing the seed types. After about five minutes, I asked each group to select a spokesperson who could share the results of their group's observations. I held up packets of seeds I had prepared to help us share our predictions. I had taped seeds from each packet to a piece of paper, which I then taped to the back of the seed packet. I held up a seed packet, walked about the room so everyone could see the seed we were talking about, and asked for group spokespersons to share their group predictions of seed types. Everyone seemed to enjoy this. I thought it was funny that, even as adults, we were intrigued by seeds. (I was surprised that few recognized the green bell pepper seed; anyone who cooks would probably be familiar with this one.)

Next, I wanted the group to dissect a seed. I held up a model drawing of a bean seed and pointed out various structures important to growing a bean plant. (I admired my handiwork—my poster drawing looked very professionally drawn!) On the model, I pointed out the seed coat, the seed leaves, and the embryo. Then, I gave each group a bowl containing beans that had been soaked overnight (this made it easier to pull the bean apart). They were to take a bean, place it on a paper plate for dissecting, and, using a toothpick, see if they could find the parts I had labeled on the model drawing.

Students had fun pulling off, as one student called it, the "seed skin." They opened up their beans. I saw some furrowed brows. Some said they couldn't find the parts that were on my model. I could see the problem. The tiny seed leaves on my picture were colored green, but the Northern beans they worked with were a solid, dull, yellow color inside and out. I let everyone dissect their bean a little longer, then passed out a worksheet which had blank label lines drawn to the seed parts I wanted them to remember. They were to look at their bean, and then color and properly label their bean seed worksheet. Few people really did this. Most pulled apart a few more beans, then discontinued the activity and threw everything in the trashcan.

For the purposes of the course assignment, I passed. I didn't, however, think the methods students really learned the bean seed parts. If only the bean seed I had used for the dissection had looked like my model drawing, then everyone could have found the right seed parts and correctly completed their worksheet.

A few weeks later, I again was a nervous mess. This time I was teaching a unit our group designed on weather to a group of second graders. We had spent three days with the group prior to this lesson, so I felt somewhat familiar with the children and their teacher. We started off the lesson by having everyone gather around a table where I was doing a "cloud making" demonstration. I set up a large glass jar covered with a piece of tin foil, and placed a pan of ice on top of the jar. I used the teacher's microwave to heat up a small jar containing water. While I was getting all the materials ready, my teaching partner was developing an "Ideas about Clouds" chart to find out what children already knew about clouds: "Clouds are white. Fluffy. Up high. Blow around. They are like cotton. They can drop rain. Fog is really a cloud on the ground." I finally had everything set up. I told the children I was going to make a cloud in a jar. I asked how many believed I could do that. I saw some perplexed faces. A few hands shot up. Some children looked a bit skeptical, but they all looked very curious. As I began to assemble the materials for the demonstration, bodies scooted forward.

Their tiny bodies began to squirm, and complain: "Hey, I was here first. I can't see! Move over!" I stopped for a moment to straighten things out—"Now look. Everyone will need to be able to see, so be careful not to block anyone's view. Some of you are way too close to the demo. I'm working with some materials I wouldn't want to spill on you, so please move back!" The children rearranged themselves, at least for three seconds. I restarted, and so did they. Every time I made a motion, there was bodily conflict within the circle group. The teacher intervened by calling a taller student to come stand by her. Once again, I tried to regain their attention.

By now, I had a small lake on top of the foil; the ice was quickly melting. The hot water was also cooling. Worse yet, rain in the jar had already begun to form and fall. The ice on top of the jar and warmer air inside was enough to make the temperature difference needed to make rain. Well, I wasn't ready for the children to see this yet, so I moved the jar off the table top, removed the ice pan, took out a new sheet of foil, and placed the materials back in view of the children.

Lifting the foil off the jar, I asked the children, "So what will happen if I pour hot water into this jar?" Students responded: "We'll see steam. The glass will fog up. The jar will get hot to touch." I responded, "Well, let's see!" I carefully poured steaming hot water into the jar. They were right on all their predictions! Next, I asked, "What do you think will happen if I put a very cold piece of foil, that's cooled by ice, on top of the jar?" I lifted out the ice resting atop the foil sheet. (I had to keep the foil on top of a paper towel to prevent it from "dripping raindrops" too soon.) An idea was offered: "The ice will melt. The solid ice will go to liquid." "Terrific, Jannell!" their classroom teacher commented. "You remembered that from our matter unit!" I was impressed! The students were quiet. They were anxious for me to put the cloud making jar into action.

As soon as I placed the ice on top of the warmed water jar, bodies were again in motion! Hands grabbed at the table top as students drew themselves nearer to see what was going on. I tried to move them a safer distance away from the demonstration area. At the same time, body wars were taking place around the perimeters of the circle. "I can't see! I can't see! Move Darron!" It was very frustrating. Not only was the demo hard for them to see inside the small jar, but with so many students seated in a small area, there was little chance of everyone even seeing the rain jar. I tried to hold up the jar so everyone could see. But then it seemed no one could see the raindrops up under the foil. I wasn't quite sure what to do. I just tried to finish up and lead the group in a discussion about their experiences with clouds.

There were many aspects of the lesson that had problems, but, again, I was disappointed in a model that was unable to help my learners see something I wanted to teach them. I am a visual person, so I believe it's really important to have visual demonstrations and drawings. However, in future lessons, I hope to find ways to involve models that work right and do what they are supposed to do!

Analysis and Discussion

1. Doloris began the bean seed lesson by using the 5-E model of teaching. If you are familiar with this model of science instruction, can you identify the various

components of the model Doloris used in her bean seed lesson? Try to revise Doloris's 5-E lesson and decide if and when a teacher-drawn model of a bean seed might best be used to support children's science learning.

2. Scientists use modeling to develop their scientific ideas. In your own words, tell what is meant by "model" and "modeling" as these relate to science teaching and learning. Doloris is incorporating the use of models into her science teaching. How does the scientist's use of a model compare and contrast with Doloris's use of models in her teaching of science? What is needed to make model use an effective aid for science teaching and learning?

3. Teacher-led demonstrations can offer exciting opportunities for group exploration of science phenomenon. On a sheet of paper divided into two columns, list some advantages and disadvantages of teacher-led science demonstrations.

4. Young children need opportunities to share ideas in large groups. Doloris's use of a large group promoted disruptive behaviors. Write some guidelines Doloris should discuss with her students to help them participate in circle or large group learning situations.

■ ■ ■

Case 2.3   Having Great and Not So Great Expectations

This is a case about a team of prospective elementary teachers teaching a science mini-unit as part of a university science methods course. The case reflects the perspective of Betsy Angleton, a classroom teacher in whose room the "methods team" taught their science mini-unit. Many problems arose when the teaching team began to teach in Betsy's classroom. This case highlights problems of differing expectations and personalities that prospective teachers bring to science teacher education.

I teach first grade in a lovely section of a large urban area. Our school has the reputation of being a school of "excellence," not only due to high scores on state tests, but because our teachers, parents, and students have high standards for teaching and learning. Many parents hold faculty positions at a nearby university. Early in January, Dr. Abernathy, a university science teacher educator, visited one of our school faculty meetings. She asked if any teachers would like to have methods students teach a science mini-unit in their classrooms. I, along with several other teachers, agreed to participate. We were given information about what we could expect from the methods students. The information sheet said the prospective teachers would:

- teach in teams of 3–4 per classroom plan and teach 4 integrated science lessons
- observe in our classroom February 17
- provide teachers with complete copies of the science mini-unit plans by February 24
- begin teaching on March 2

Dr. Abernathy provided her phone number in case we had questions or problems. We were asked to provide a topic for their science unit planning and teaching. I told her that the topic for my first grade class needed to fit in with the theme: "Looking Above and Below." More specifically, they could focus on studying the ground and rocks around us.

As planned, the teaching team, four young women, arrived to observe my classroom on February 17. I'd rearranged my lesson plans for the morning so that they could observe science taking place. Since we were finishing a unit on "Things of Long Ago," they observed the students making dioramas of prehistoric landscapes. I greeted the team, and asked them to introduce themselves to the class. I told my students the university science team would return in a few weeks to lead science time. Before leaving, one of the team members, Donna, said she would bring the unit for me to review on February 22. I told her we were going on a field trip that day to the Natural History Museum, but that it would be all right for her to leave it in my mailbox. We planned to meet on February 24 during my conference period so I could share feedback on the unit with the team.

Later, I looked over the unit. Basically, I was pleased with the integrated science activities they had planned. The team had included ways to find out what the children might already know about soil and rocks, fun hands-on science activities that clearly related to the concepts to be learned, and a selection of two children's books that would be wonderful springboards for introducing and reinforcing ideas. I wrote a few comments to suggest management strategies, and alterations needed for data collection worksheets (too much text written on a couple of the sheets would overwhelm my young readers). The methods team met with me on February 24 to review the unit; everyone was there except one person, Ashley. No one seemed to know why she was not present and we waited for a few minutes in case she was running late. After 10 minutes, we decided to go ahead and discuss the unit. I reviewed my written comments with the team. They asked if I had a few materials they could use, and then left—very excited about teaching in nearly one week!

On March 2, three of the four methods students arrived in my classroom about 10 minutes early. My students were working on handwriting, so the team began to set up materials. It was soon time for the science lesson to begin, so Donna led the children to the carpeted area of the room and introduced herself and the rest of the teaching team: "Good morning. My name is Ms. Donna, this is Ms. Jarrell, and Ms. Crystal. One teacher is not here yet, but she should arrive soon! Let's go ahead and get started." She then began to read a book, *Everybody Needs a Rock,* by Byrd Baylor, to the class.

Nearly five minutes late, the fourth member of the teaching team, Ashley, arrived. She slid beside the other team members leaning against a table near the carpet area. Ms. Donna, who was reading the book, paused, looked up at the late team member and said to the students: "Ah, our fourth teacher has arrived. This is Ms. Ashley." The children turned to look at Ashley. In the moment of distraction, while the children's heads were turned, Donna opened her eyes wide and glared very hard at Ashley. She stated somewhat tersely: "In just a few minutes, when we finish sharing our book, Ms. Ashley is going to lead us in an exciting activity. Right, Ms. Ashley?" Ashley, looking a bit surprised, replied, "Well, um, right. I'll get things ready now." Ms. Donna regained the children's attention and resumed reading the book to them. Ashley nervously walked over to me and said, "Mrs. Angleton, I must apologize. I didn't realize today was my day to teach. I thought we were to teach this lesson on Day Two. Do you have any containers—cups or buckets, and a small shovel or spoon?" I tried to be gracious, but I began to feel heat moving up my neck and my face turned red. I felt both frustrated at and embarrassed for this young woman. I told her, "Well, I have a bucket and a garden trowel. Will those help?" Ms. Ashley responded, "Ah, yes. Great! Perhaps I need one more thing—newspaper." I showed her a large stack of newspapers in a corner of the classroom. Ms. Ashley quickly got the newspapers. She directed Crystal to spread the newspapers across the student's tables, and to put a stack of blank sheets of paper and crayons in the center of each table. Accompanied by Jarrell, Ashley slipped out the back door with a bucket and trowel in hand. In the meantime, Dr. Abernathy came in the room to see how things were going for the teaching team. I waved to her briefly as she stood beside Crystal at the table. They exchanged whispers, and I could see Dr. Abernathy's face change; her eyebrows were furrowed. Ms. Donna finished reading the book. To explore some ideas the children had about rocks, she created a K–W–L (Know, Want to Know, Learned) chart. Just as the children finished listing questions under the "W—What Would You Like to Know?" section of the chart, Ashley and Jarrell returned with a bucket full of sand collected from the schoolyard. Ashley quickly put sand in small piles on the newspaper at places where the children would be seated. Donna said to the group, "Terrific. Ms. Ashley is all ready. She will now tell us what we are to do next." Ashley stood at the carpet edge and told the children: "I want you to go back to your table seat. When you get there, look carefully at the sand. On the sheet of paper, I want you to draw what you see." The children followed her directions. They quickly found their seats. Their tiny fingers sifted through the sand. The teaching team milled about the tables, asking children what they were seeing. Already, it was time to clean up! I told the children to carefully fold up the newspapers and put them in the trash. It was time to go to art class. I led the line of children out the door, and said I would be back in just a minute to talk with the team.

Dr. Abernathy asked us all to gather around a table. "Does anyone want to share some insights to help us understand what took place in here today?" Donna hesitantly spoke first: "Well, what actually happened isn't what we expected to have happen." Dr. Abernathy looked at me and asked, "Mrs. Angleton, would you please tell us what you thought about today's lesson?" I wasn't quite sure what to say. "Well, to be honest, I'm not sure what happened. We reviewed the unit plans and today's lesson didn't go according to plan. The story reading was fine, but the rock investigation didn't take place as planned. Today's lesson was supposed to use rocks, but it ended up being the soil exploration lesson." I hesitated for a moment and then said firmly to the team members, "You were not prepared today. My first graders may seem like little children to you and you might assume they don't see it, but they do. You were not ready to challenge their thinking. Unless you can offer my students a meaningful science experience, please do not return to teach in this classroom. I'm very sorry, but that's how I feel!" Dr. Abernathy looked quite frustrated. She was silent for a moment, then stated: "You were given instructions and examples for submitting lesson plans to the classroom teacher. I don't understand why a lesson plan was not available for today's teaching session. It appears that this group, for some reason, did not plan together for today's teaching. Let's try to figure out what went wrong so we can be better prepared to teach next time."

There was a pause, then Donna spoke hesitantly, "I hate to say anything because I know we are all responsible. I'm a quiet type of person and I avoid getting into arguments. To be honest, though, I've found it hard to work with this team because some members dominate the group, and others just go along with things. We couldn't seem to agree on anything to teach for these lessons. I'm very picky about details. I felt like we should plan everything out and double check to be sure everyone was ready, but others didn't see it that way. I felt like I was being a nag, so I just shut up."

Crystal, with tears welling up in her eyes, began to cry: "I'm so sorry about all this. I feel terrible. I didn't really check to see what today's plans were because I knew it wasn't my day to teach. I'm not accustomed to using lesson plans. The teacher I observe for my internship never really uses lesson plans, she just seems to wing it. I guess I thought we were winging it today or something." "Winging it?" Dr. Abernathy responded, "How long has your teacher been teaching?" Crystal replied, "About 21 years I think." "Well," Dr. Abernathy said, "Maybe 'winging it' is how it appears in a teacher with 21 years of experience. You are not that experienced yet. Planning is especially important since you are working as a team to teach these lessons. Today, your team apparently did not work as a team." Ashley, looking somewhat offended, said a bit angrily, "Well, I'm sorry about today but I just didn't know what was going on! I'm quite busy with a lot of things now, and, well, no one bothered to tell me that today's lesson had been changed from what we'd originally planned!" Dr. Abernathy turned toward Ashley and said: "Well, that's a problem, it's a real problem that you expected someone to tell you! Why weren't you available to ask about plans?"

Observing all this taking place, I saw several problems. Here was a group of four pre-service teachers who didn't seem to understand how much planning it takes to teach science. They have observed teachers who have years of experience teaching and have no idea what it has taken for these teachers to develop the fluid knowledge and apparent ease in teaching students. I wanted to help this group, but I could see they struggled to work together. Dr. Abernathy asked if I would permit the team to continue teaching in my classroom. I said that I would, but that I expected them to be prepared with a well-organized plan. Dr. Abernathy left, but the teaching team remained a few minutes longer to go over the mini-unit plans. With a few adjustments, they left with definite roles and goals in mind for teaching the next science lesson. For the sake of my students, as well as these novice teachers, I hoped the group could work through their differences to successfully team teach the science unit.

Analysis and Discussion

1. What key factors contributed to the problems the teaching team faced on Day One?

2. Teachers are often asked to work as grade-level teaching teams. In this case, the teammates had differing expectations, which hampered the effectiveness of their instruction in the classroom. What can be done to prevent personality conflicts when you are asked to work on a team? To brainstorm ideas, divide a paper into two columns. In one column, list possible reasons for conflict, and, in the second column, write down strategies that might be taken to prevent or to address conflicts.

3. Imagine that you are one of the student teachers, Ashley, Donna, Crystal, or Jarrell. What would you have done following the unit review meeting on February 24 to prevent the kind of communication gaps that Ashley perceived to be a problem? What would you have done on March 2 when Ashley did not arrive on time?

4. The group ran into problems by not having the proper materials needed to teach the first lesson. What sorts of materials would you gather in advance to be prepared for teaching this unit on soil and rocks?

5. Donna used a K-W-L (Know, Want to Know, Learned) chart as an advance organizer for teaching the unit. What if you constructed a K-W-L chart and discovered that your students already knew the concepts you had planned to teach in your unit? What would you do? What other sorts of strategies besides a K-W-L chart could be used to find out what children know?

■ ■ ■

Case 2.4   But We've Always Done It This Way

Field experiences for prospective teachers are sometimes precarious arrangements. Prospective teachers are placed in classrooms with unfamiliar teachers and students, and often are expected to assume teaching responsibilities immediately. In this case, a prospective teacher named Nicky is assigned to be an intern in Diana's fourth grade classroom. Diana has established practices of teaching and learning that shape what happens when Nicky tries to teach. This case, written by Nicky, focuses on some of the problems she experienced learning to teach science during her internship experience.

Nearly one year ago, I was a senior enrolled in elementary teacher education at Bellmore University. I'd completed the first year of the program, and was beginning the internship semester. For the most part, I felt ready to begin teaching. Others who had gone before me said that the placement of interns and student teachers with classroom teachers was basically a "blind" process. I understood that to mean that neither the cooperating teacher nor the prospective teacher knew anything about each other prior to committing to work with each other. They warned me that, in the placement process, sometimes you got lucky and sometimes you didn't. I was quite nervous about this. What if I got placed with a teacher who had old-fashioned teaching methods? What if she wouldn't let me try out my own ideas? What if the students in her classroom didn't like me?

At the beginning of the fall semester, I submitted my internship paperwork, then waited to find out where, and with whom, I would be placed. Finally, word came from the College of Education Placement Office. They had arranged for me to meet Diana Morris, a fourth grade teacher at Cherry Hill Elementary.

It was early September. As I drove out to meet Diana during her morning conference period, I was nervous. What if I sensed right away that the teacher and I would not be a good match? Could I request a different cooperating teacher? I found my way to Diana's classroom. I walked into room 21 and said, "Hi, are you Mrs. Morris?" "Yes, I am. Hello! Are you my intern? Come on in and have a seat. And please, call me Diana." She smiled, extended her hand to shake mine, and invited me to sit with her at a table. Her students were at art class, so we had about 25 minutes to talk.

We briefly shared information about ourselves. Diana told me that this was her third year of teaching. She had received a master's degree in elementary education, and loved being a fourth grade teacher. She told me, with an obvious sense of pride, that she was full-blooded Cherokee. (Not to sound stereotypical, but she reminded me of the character in the Walt Disney movie "Pocahontas." She was strikingly beautiful.) On the bulletin board were symbols representing Indian language. I noticed a "book of the week" placed at a reading table area; it was *The Education of Little Tree*. I noted aloud, "You have a lot of interesting Indian artifacts around your room." "Yes," she replied, "We will be studying all sorts of cultural groups this year. Indian groups are featured throughout Fall—I introduce my own Cherokee background, then we talk about Florida Seminoles in our state history unit, and then expand to talk about Indians and pilgrims in November. The kids really love learning about Indians. They come to understand that we are not riding around in canoes and living in tepees these days!" I laughed. She was intriguing.

I shared a bit about myself too; I'm a much less colorful character in comparison to Diana. I've lived in this city all my life, and grew up knowing that I would someday graduate from Bellmore University. My father runs a major office supply store in town. I love riding horses. I especially love the outdoors. As I think about teaching, I think it's why I'm most enthusiastic about teaching science.

Diana and I negotiated a schedule that would allow me to visit her classroom 2 and ½ days per week, for a 10-week period. I also needed to complete two weeks of total teaching time (i.e., to assume full responsibility for the classroom) by mid-November. I had brought my lists of assignments and due dates to review with Diana. There were interviews to be carried out with teachers and students, math diagnostic tests to be performed with each student in the classroom, and planning and teaching of a two-week thematic unit by mid-November. "No problem!" she said,

"We'll clear this table and you can make it your own desk area. Feel free to call back students as you need them. I know what it's like trying to get all those university assignments done on time. It's hard work!" We talked for a few more minutes, exchanged telephone numbers, and then I left. I really looked forward to doing my internship in Diana's classroom! In late September, I received notice that my internship placement in Diana's classroom had officially been approved. I was thrilled!

September 22

I made my first visit to Diana's classroom to make initial observations. Diana had cleared a table on the side of the classroom where I could keep my belongings, and work on my assignment tasks. Sitting at the table I could easily observe her classroom without getting in anyone's way. Diana's classroom had about 26 students. It was a relaxed atmosphere. The student's desks were arranged in several clusters, with desktops touching each other; it was like having little neighborhoods of students about the room.

The students were in the process of doing what Diana called "Indian math." (Actually, it was a pre-algebra-type activity in which Indian symbols were used to represent an unknown number in their math problems.) Diana finished reviewing the math concept her students would be working on that day, and, before handing out a math worksheet, briefly introduced me to the group. I smiled, stood, and told the group, "Hi. I'm very glad to be here. I look forward to teaching all of you this semester!" I sat down and continued to observe the group at work.

The math worksheet was passed out to the students, and they quickly got to work. There was little or no talking. I was impressed. They were such worker bees! Diana had seated herself at her desk, and apparently was marking papers. Over the next 45 minutes, children silently completed their work, then either found other worksheets to work on or colored pictures at their desk. They were a smooth running machine! Everyone clearly knew they were expected to focus on, and complete, their tasks. On each visit to the classroom, I observed the eagerness of these students to work. How did Diana do it? How did she get them to work so easily?

I quickly developed my own routines when I visited the classroom. I would: arrive, take out my university assignments, prioritize which ones I should work on, and then "pull students" from Diana's class to work with me on assignment tasks. About two weeks into the internship, I wrote in my personal journal:

October 17

It is so sad that since my first day, and the days that have followed, I have been so busy with getting methods assignments done, I feel I get only glimpses of what's going on in the classroom. I haven't had any time to talk with Diana or to observe while she teaches. I'm just so busy and stressed about getting my university course assignments completed. Every 10 minutes or so, I try to glance up to see what's going on. I know about the students' need to learn note-taking skills. And I see how she organizes students to do their work by putting assignments up on the board. She uses a reward system of giving her students extra minutes outdoors if they complete work quickly as a group, or for when they behave extra well. I just wish I didn't feel so distracted and pressured to get all these methods class assignments done.

After a couple of weeks, I began to assume more teaching responsibilities in the classroom. I needed to get as much teaching experience as I possibly could get; I wanted to be ready for the two-week "total teach" I'd have to do. I helped to monitor students as they worked on worksheets, and I walked students to and from other classes and lunch. I also got to take them outdoors for "free time." Free time was the carrot Diana used to motivate her students to do their work. For every minute that the entire class finished their in-class worksheets ahead of schedule, they earned a minute of free time. This contract was a very effective way of encouraging the students' cooperation and participation in the classroom!

As time progressed, Diana become preoccupied with a lot of things and was becoming less and less available to me. Evidently, she'd been given a major role on a school committee, the site-management team. During planning or lunch periods, Diana was either on the phone in the corner of her classroom, or busy talking with other faculty members in other classrooms. Initially, this didn't bother me. Diana's absence gave me a chance to take charge of the classroom, and I took on the role of teaching the entire class often.

The university had required that Diana, my university supervisor, and I maintain a dialogue journal (a journal we each could write in to share ideas). We really didn't write in it too often, but Diana tried to write at least one entry each week in the journal. One day, about the fourth week I was there, she wrote:

> I really like having someone else to learn with. This is only my third year of teaching, so I need to get more teaching ideas. I get very few opportunities like this to see someone else's ideas. I just wish I could focus on teaching. We have all this school-based management stuff now. To be honest, since I'm their token minority, they put me on all sorts of committees. It's hard to keep up with everything, much less my classroom teaching responsibilities! I'm writing all this, wondering, are you doing okay, Nicky? Am I abandoning you too much?

About that same time, I had written in my personal journal:

November 2

I wish we [Diana and I] could talk more. She's like a greased pig—hard to catch! There are so many people always coming in and out of the room wanting to talk with her about their team things and getting the computer stuff organized. I know Diana appreciates me being here so that she can have someone to share teaching ideas with; she doesn't feel there is anyone else at her stage (in career) to talk with about teaching. But since she is so preoccupied with other school problems, we just don't get any time to talk.

I didn't feel comfortable telling Diana I needed her attention; she obviously had many pressures coming from all directions. I decided that I should make the best of the situation. I began to plan and try out different teaching strategies I'd been taught at the university. Of all the teaching strategies I learned, cooperative group work was the one I most wanted to try out. I had asked Diana in our dialogue journal if I could use cooperative grouping. She wrote back:

November 7:

I haven't used cooperative learning this year yet. I'm still in the process of helping them learn to work with partners. I think it's a really good idea, but my experience has been that cooperative learning always seems to leave someone out. There's always someone who's the leader, and someone who's a follower. I know I should go around and assign everybody a job in their group, but I just don't think that's realistic. There are always going to be those people who try to manipulate everyone else's work. In our lives there are people who feel it is their job to control everyone else, and others who give in to this. Whether they work in groups of two, three or five—someone is going to be an imposition on someone else. But give it a try! You might know some ways that will make larger groupings a great success. I'll look forward to watching and learning from you!

It was getting close to the time for my two-week total teaching session to begin, so I started taking opportunities to get the students working in cooperative groups. Initially, the students seemed to like that idea. But as soon as they would start to work in their groups, fussing and fighting would immediately follow. They did not want to share materials and they couldn't seem to organize themselves to work together. Everyone wanted to be the Materials Manager, or Principal Investigator. No one would be a Recorder or Reporter. Disagreements and disruptive behavior escalated quickly. I was unsure of how to cope with the increasing noise and outbursts of the students. The class was getting behind on their assignments because we had to keep stopping work to deal with the problems that were undermining their activities. Students said I was a real "whip cracker," a "slave driver." I didn't like these descriptions of my role as a teacher. What happened to my image of being a facilitator? When I asked why their groups were not getting along, one student replied: "We don't like it when you keeping telling us to hurry up and finish. I could get things done faster when I worked alone." Other students added their complaints: "I don't like doing group work; it slows us down." "You're not letting us finish our work, so we aren't able to earn free time outside." "Why can't we do like we were doing, working by ourselves?" I felt confused and frustrated. I thought they would really like working in groups. I also thought the hands-on activities supported a much higher level of learning than the worksheets. What was I doing, or not doing, that was making the cooperative group work unsuccessful?

I decided that one problem was that these students didn't know the difference between doing work and doing science learning. I decided I would continue to teach the students in cooperative learning groups; these students just needed time to give it a try. I also changed the "Fun Friday" reward system. Every week ended with a "Fun Friday," a half-day of video watching and popcorn eating. Last week they watched "Robin Hood." I thought some of the content of the movie was quite "adult" in nature, and I didn't see any benefit to their learning through watching the film. To me, "Fun Friday" just seemed to be a waste of time. I wanted them to really learn something, and to show them that learning could be fun!

For two Fridays, instead of "Fun Friday," I set up several "bubbleology" centers for them to explore. I thought this would be great—they could learn science and have fun at the same time. The students really enjoyed the bubbles. They tried to make square and triangle bubbles using pipe cleaners. They experimented making bubbles using different brands of dishwashing soap. And they tried to blow bubbles inside of bubbles. The most impressive center was a small plastic wading pool filled with liquid soup. The students could stand in it (on top of a stool) and pull a huge bubble up over their body using a hula hoop as a giant bubble wand. They groaned when I asked them later to write about their experiences in their science journal. One student wrote: "The bubbles were fun, but I missed having Fun Friday. We work hard to get Fun Friday. Please let us start having our points so we can get free time and Fun Fridays back." I didn't understand. They felt I had taken away their free time. They were resenting this changed deal; I'd broken the work contract.

That evening, I wrote in my personal journal:

December 2

I don't understand. The students seemed to really enjoy the bubbles, but they'd rather watch videos and eat popcorn. I have a problem with that. Fun Fridays seem like such a waste of time. I think it's important for kids to have fun in school, but they can learn to have fun through learning. I only have one more week of total-teach, and then it will be over. I'm not going to do any more cooperative groups or set up centers. It's apparent to me that Diana and these kids have worked out a deal. The goal, under Diana's teaching and learning "contract" was to get work accomplished; I misunderstood, thinking the goal was to get learning to take place.

My final week, I reinstated the worksheet and punch clock regimen. It worked like magic. The children were once again happily working side by side, helping each other as needed, and finishing their work. On my last day of visiting the classroom, they devoted Fun Friday toward hosting a Good Luck party in my honor.

Analysis and Discussion

1. Nicky and Diana had different philosophies about student work and student learning. Describe and compare the views of Nicky and Diana with regard to their ideas about teaching and learning. How do their views compare to your own notions about teaching and learning science?

2. What were the students' assumptions and expectations about teaching and learning?

3. What do you believe should serve as motivation for students' science learning? What roles can you play toward encouraging students' motivation to learn science?

4. Lack of communication was one problem in this case. What, if anything, might Nicky have done to establish better communication between herself and Diana?

5. There is no mention of the role the university supervisor played during Nicky's internship, and Diana's role as cooperating teacher seemed to be ill-defined. What roles do you think the university supervisor and cooperating teacher should have in supporting the intern's learning about teaching? How might these be negotiated before and during internship or student teaching experiences?

■ ■ ■

Case 2.5   Weathering the Storm

Cathy is a student teacher who has just completed one month of student teaching in Mrs. Gladworth's kindergarten classroom. In this case, Cathy describes her role in teaching the children about daily weather events. Her task becomes complicated when several hurricanes have devastating effects in their area. Cathy is also challenged as she tries to help a non-English-speaking child understand what has taken place.

For the past month, I have been student teaching in Mrs. Gladworth's kindergarten classroom. It has been exciting to see how five-year-olds view the world around them. We have 25 children in our classroom, two of whom are from other countries. Kanon is one of these; his family came to the United States only two weeks before school started. They had fled from Bosnia and resided in a refugee camp in Germany before coming here. Kanon, like most other students, arrived bright-eyed and enthusiastic about learning in kindergarten last August! Although he spoke no English, Kanon seemed comfortable in the warm atmosphere of Mrs. Gladworth's classroom. Centers for art, block building, dramatic play, listening and writing, and several others, painted red, yellow, blue and green, presented an inviting sight for everyone who entered the classroom!

We spent a great deal of time those first weeks helping the children learn the class routines. Mrs. Gladworth emphasized children helping each other (which I quickly came to appreciate, as it's hard to have 25 students depending on you for their every need!). One routine the children quickly looked forward to was gathering together for Focus Time. After a brief journal writing time (which really was more like picture drawing time), Mrs. Gladworth called all the students over to the carpet area for Focus Time. If they wanted, children could share about what they had "written" in their journals. After some initial discussions, we would then teach or review various topics. One topic we focused on at the start of the year were days of the week, and using numbers to count days. While most of the children already knew how to count aloud, they were less familiar with the idea of connecting numeric symbols with spoken numbers. Another topic, which I was soon given responsibility to review during Focus Time, was the daily weather.

We had a weather graph that showed pictures of various weather phenomena, and words on cards that could be matched up and placed below the pictures. There were cards for sunny, cloudy, rainy and foggy weather. Each day, we sent children to the window area to observe the sky. The students would describe what they saw, then select a card and place it below the corresponding picture on the weather graph that best matched their descriptions. It was wise that Mrs. Gladworth sent the children in pairs to carry out this task—especially when it was the non-English-speaking students' turn. One morning, when Kanon was called on to tell us about the weather, he had a very anxious look. He had heard his name called, but wasn't quite sure why. He looked greatly relieved when a partner grabbed his hand and led him over to the window to check the weather. The children were great about helping each other follow along, and I was particularly glad to see this on behalf of Kanon. He was very shy among the other children and spoke very little, but they were eager to help him when he did not seem to understand things, and he responded happily to work with them.

During the fall season, learning about weather in some regions of the United States can be quite exciting—particularly when hurricanes develop! Our reports got very interesting as Hurricane Dennis approached, went out to sea, and then returned again to our region. Since we live about 100 miles inland, Hurricane Dennis was not a serious threat. We experienced a bit of rainfall and gusty winds; our school closed twice until Dennis finally passed. Nearly one week later, television reports showed the development of a huge hurricane, Hurricane Floyd, and it was heading our way! All week long, television reports and newspaper headlines warned about the oncoming "Fury of Floyd." As Floyd neared land, our skies became quite dark. On Wednesday afternoon, heavy rains from the oncoming hurricane were already making it difficult to travel on the roads. Mrs. Gladworth and I both felt quite nervous wondering what sort of impact this storm would have; the children seemed to have little awareness of the potential danger Hurricane Floyd posed.

Thursday, the hurricane hit our area. As I listened to weather updates on a portable radio, reports indicated that our entire area had flooded beyond what anyone would imagine possible. People's homes were filled with water as rivers and creeks filled and overflowed their boundaries. I could hear helicopters flying throughout the next day and night as hundreds of people were rescued from the dangerous waters. I was very fortunate; my own apartment was high and dry.

Our schools were closed for over a week as schools across the entire eastern region of the state were being used as emergency shelters. Over a week later, faculty in our district were required to return to school. We spent part of Thursday and Friday preparing for the return of our students. As we talked, we were both worried about helping our students understand the natural disaster that had taken place. We wondered if many of their homes had been flooded. My thoughts turned to Kanon. He had been through a tremendous ordeal already; how would he deal with the devastation of the floods? Mrs. Gladworth encouraged me to think of a tangible way I might help the children talk about the flooded rivers and to see what had taken place to cause the massive floods. How could I simulate the disaster that had taken place in a way they could understand? I wanted them to talk about their experiences, but I also wanted to avoid re-traumatizing them as they recalled what happened.

That evening, I searched the World Wide Web to look for suggestions to help me teach about natural disasters. I typed in the key words "Floods" and "Teaching" and a number of websites were suggested. One site was really excellent. It had suggestions for teaching about hurricanes, tornadoes, fires, and floods. The site on floods suggested reading a children's book entitled *Come a Tide* by George Ella Lyon. The book would be perfect as it talked about spring floods taking place in a rural area! I wondered, however, if I could find a way to actually show what had happened.

I decided to make a model to show how floods take place. I spent most of Friday morning assembling materials. I got a copy of the book from our university library, and then worked on a flood model. At first, I tried using a cardboard box, but the water quickly softened the box and it fell apart. I then tried using a large plastic tub. I lined the bottom of the tub with two large pieces of foil and poured a great deal of sand into each section; the foil helped hold the sand back so that I could form a river down the center of the tub. I cut some sections of grass from our lawn to lay over the sand. I also cut a few sprigs from a bush to serve as trees, and painted some of the leaves red and orange to give them a fall-like appearance. I used a few wooden shapes that looked like houses and placed these about the tub. It looked terrific! It looked just like a small town with a river flowing through it!

School resumed on Monday. Most of our children had been safe throughout the storm, and 22 of our 25 students showed up for class that morning. We didn't tell the children to journal about anything in particular; as usual, they wrote or drew as they wished. Once everyone had gotten settled in, we gathered the children for Focus Time at the carpet area.

Mrs. Gladworth began by reviewing the last day everyone had been together. She talked about how it had been rainy. We placed "X"s on the days between that date and the current date, and then counted how many days we had missed school. We had missed eight days of school! She then encouraged the children to talk about what they heard, what they saw, and what they felt. The children shared their pictures and stories. Overall, our students seemed to have little anxiety about the situation. Most drew rainy pictures. A few students talked about having relatives whose homes had flooded, but no one in our class had experienced any direct damage from the hurricane. Kanon had drawn a picture of a tree laying against his home. I asked him about his picture; he quietly said, "It was okay." Almost everyone said they were glad to be back at school as it had gotten boring at home.

I read *Come A Tide* to the group. They anxiously talked about seeing homes underwater on television, and some shared stories about friends they knew who had to move because of the flooding. There was mention of the "monster" hurricane. It was an excellent time to involve them in making a model of how flooding takes place. I explained that hurricanes aren't monsters (although news reports had called it a "monster hurricane"), they are natural events. I then had the students take turns making it rain on the small town using small bottles of water. It rained and rained and rained. It rained until the small river became quite deep. It rained until the river overflowed its banks. Students eyes became large and they squealed as the river began to rise up on the small houses. The houses were covered until water reached the roof lines. Then the rains stopped.

I reviewed with the students what had taken place; I wanted to be sure they understood the idea of flooding. I looked directly at Kanon. I pointed to the high water in the model and asked him, "What is this, Kanon?" His eyes lit up, he plunged his finger into the waters around the houses and said loudly, "Flood." He got it! I was thrilled!

Using physical situations, such as watching the sky, and physical models such as our flood in a tub, really played a significant role toward helping our students understand their daily world. Our science learning helped students, including Kanon, develop literacy and social links as well! While I've always thought science was interesting, I now believe this type of science teaching will be a highlight in my future classroom.

Analysis and Discussion

1. What is the main point of this case?

2. To what extent should a classroom be a safe haven for children from a confusing and sometimes dangerous world as opposed to a place where they learn to cope with the "real world"?

3. What other kinds of weather or weather-related events might young children have difficulty understanding?

4. Develop some teacher guidelines for using models and modeling processes to teach science.

5. In this case, the student teacher is learning about helping young children develop literacy skills through her science teaching. What relationships do you see between science literacy and reading literacy?

6. Mrs. Gladworth integrated language arts, mathematics and science into what she called "Focus Time." The integration of science into other subject areas is less commonly practiced in intermediate and higher grade levels. Why do you think this is so? What are some advantages and disadvantages for integrating science into other subject areas in instruction?

7. Students in Mrs. Gladworth's classroom were encouraged to help each other instead of relying on a teacher's assistance. We saw an example of this when Kanon's partner automatically grabbed his hand to involve him in giving the weather report. What can teachers do at the beginning of the school year to encourage students to help each other? How can teachers help students be more autonomous in their science learning?

Case 2.6   Surfing into a Science Research Quandary

Michelle Chen was a student teacher at Indian Hills Elementary School, a suburban elementary school located in an area that serves middle- and lower-income families. The school had about 400 students, with nearly forty percent African-American, fifty percent

Caucasian, and a few students who were Hispanic and Asian. Michelle's case involves the use of multiple information sources to support teaching about endangered animals. She set up multiple learning centers, including one that involved searching (i.e., "surfing") Internet websites. Problems arose as children obtained inconsistent information through the different information resources used. Questions about appropriate use of technology resources, determining the accuracy of scientific information, and the tentative nature of science are considered in this case.

The fifth grade classroom in which I taught had two computers that were connected to the Internet. My supervising teacher, Mrs. Cannon, had not used the classroom computers as an actual part of instruction, and taught science two afternoons a week using only the science textbook. I knew that I wanted to teach science differently than Mrs. Cannon had been teaching it. I talked with her to see if she would allow me to use a different approach to teach science, and she offered to support me in whatever new directions I might take.

I developed a science unit about "Endangered Animals" that involved student learning through the use of research, cooperative groups, and learning centers. One learning center featured the use of Internet web browsers on our classroom computers; I called this the "Internet Learning Center." Additional learning centers were set up with other resources, including children's literature about endangered animals, encyclopedias, magazines with pictures students could cut out, an endangered animal species game, and a collection of state wildlife brochures. I assigned all students to cooperative groups, and let each group select a specific animal to research. Each group was given a research grid to structure their work. The grid asked for information that included:

- Name of animal (including genus and species)
- Where it lives
- What it eats
- Predators
- Current population
- Major cause of its endangerment
- Ways we might help the animal survive

All groups spent the first day deciding on an endangered animal to research. Students selected animals from a list I had received from a national wildlife organization. After a brief introduction about endangered animals, the groups began working on their research at the various learning centers. The students worked smoothly at most centers; however, the Internet Learning Center did introduce some unique problems.

Only one group at a time was permitted to use the Internet Learning Center for a maximum of one day of science time (I taught science for one hour each day for two weeks). Groups worked in pairs (or singly if a group had only three members) taking turns searching bookmarked sites I had prepared in advance. At one point, I heard loud laughter from a pair working at a computer and checked to see what they were looking at onscreen. Somehow, the "Bear" group had accessed a pornographic web site. I reprimanded the students for wandering "offsite" and quickly tried to exit the web page they had found, but the site must have been programmed in some special way—it was impossible to turn off! I had to shut down the computer and restart the entire system. One child's parent called Mrs. Cannon at home that evening and said: "I heard about the 'miseducative' experience that took place in your classroom today during science time. I do not want my daughter to use the Internet without direct adult supervision." Mrs. Cannon told me about the phone call the next day in class, and offered to supervise students while they worked at the Internet Learning Center. That was great, but it made me wonder—what would I do in the future if I were teaching alone in the classroom and wanted to involve children in web surfing?

Students tried to use information from the different resources at the other centers. Our science text provided little or no information about animals they had selected. The state wildlife brochure center was helpful to some groups, but only those who had selected animals living in our region of the U.S. One group researching the American peregrine falcon found information in the state wildlife brochure to be inconsistent with information they found on the Internet. The brochure indicated that their animal was on the "Endangered Species" list, whereas the web site they accessed did not list the animal on the state Endangered Species list. Things got more complicated when a parent of one of the students, a local park ranger, visited our class to give a presentation about endangered animals. After sharing information about endangered animals and his work as a park ranger, he responded to questions from students. One student tried to get clarification for his group's report:

> Kelly: Is the peregrine falcon endangered?
> Park Ranger parent: Yes. That animal has been endangered for quite some time now.
> Kelly: I'm just asking because our group has researched the falcon. It was listed on the endangered animal list we got from our teacher. Then we looked up information on a state list—from the brochures table—and it listed the falcon on the state endangered list. Then we looked it up on the Internet. The web page we used showed endangered animals for our state, but it said nothing about the falcon. So, is our animal endangered or not?
> Park Ranger: Well, it depends on where that information has come from I guess. I can tell you that the peregrine falcon is still a very endangered animal in our region. Another question?

Later, after the park ranger had left the classroom, Kelly still wondered which source to use for his research:

> Kelly: Ms. Chen, we're still not sure which answer is right. Should we go with the park ranger, the park booklets, or the Internet information?
> Ms. Chen: Well, which source do you think is most likely to be right?
> Kelly: I think the information on the Internet.
> Ms. Chen: Why?

Kelly: I'm not sure, but that information is probably newer. It just looks newer than our science book or the park booklets.

Ms. Chen: How do you decide if information you read or hear is accurate?

Another student, Purvi: Well, the information we've been looking up is science information. I guess people who know this sort of information are the ones who write it on the websites. A park ranger isn't a scientist, so I don't think he really knew the right answer about your animal, Kelly.

I was feeling quite uncomfortable at this point. Tommy, whose father was the park ranger, looked rather anxious as the knowledge of his father was questioned. Also, I wasn't sure how up-to-date the information on the Internet might be. Furthermore, I wasn't sure how data is collected about animal populations and then used to determine when a particular species is endangered. And, finally, how appropriate is it for me to suggest to these fifth graders that science information they get isn't always right?

Analysis and Discussion

1. In what ways does using the Internet for science teaching and learning compare with instruction based solely on the use of printed text materials? Create a chart to list advantages and disadvantages for both instructional approaches.

2. What assumptions do the students have about where science knowledge comes from and who is a scientist?

3. At the end of the case, Ms. Chen asks " . . . how appropriate is it for me to suggest to these fifth graders that science information they get isn't always right?" In one sense she may be asking when students should be taught about the tentative nature of science. Alternatively, she may be considering how the students felt as they questioned whether or not to accept Tommy's father's response. How did you interpret her question, and what is your response?

4. What sorts of science inquiry activities could be used to help children understand how scientists gather data about animal communities and populations?

5. Ms. Chen experienced some difficulty managing children's use of the Internet. What strategies would you use to encourage proper use of computer tools (e.g., interactive learning games, multimedia software) in the classroom? More specifically, how would you monitor children's use of the Internet to prevent miseducative experiences as seen in this case?

6. Imagine that your school has received money to purchase computer technology resources to be used specifically for teaching science. Your grade level has been given $3,000 to spend for this purpose. Where could you get information to use so that your team could generate a "wish list" of science technology resources? What criteria would you use to select "good" science learning technology tools?

3

Creating an Environment
for Learning Science

You may have a mental picture of a good science teacher as one who manages the routines, the equipment, the planning and explanation of each day's classroom activities so that children move about purposefully, talk quietly and cooperate in sharing materials and taking turns. While this is a very attractive picture and an ideal to strive for, like other ideals, it is seldom, if ever, attained in the real world. Children don't always behave as we want them to, accidents happen and sometimes materials that are needed aren't available. What do you do when a child says "No" or hits you? It can happen. The cases in this chapter will show you how other teachers have responded to these problems and will help you make decisions about what to do when you confront similar situations.

Two of the cases in this chapter deal with a student's unacceptable behavior and the teacher's dilemma about the best way to handle the problem. Notice that we did not say "the right way" to handle the problem; problems of this kind do not have one and only one correct solution and it may be better to think of resolving a situation rather than solving a problem. Whatever action is taken, the teacher has to think of the consequences for the other children as well as for the disruptive child. In one case, there were unexpected consequences for the teacher as well.

Another case deals with a problem that is inevitable and only partly within the teacher's control, the problem of children spilling things on the floor. This is a minor problem in a room with a wooden floor, but when science is taught in a carpeted room, it's a different story, as you will see. Obtaining and maintaining the special equipment and materials needed for science presents a third kind of management problem, the subject of another case.

Management, whether of materials or of classroom behavior, should never be your main concern in teaching science; it is only important as a means to an end. However, it *is* important because children can't work productively and learn in a classroom where their classmates are out of control, where necessary materials are not available and where a spill is a major disaster. We have placed this chapter focusing on management before the chapter focusing on instruction to remind you that the management issues raised by these teachers must be dealt with in order to have an effective and exciting activity-based science program.

3.1

I Won't Sit with Girls

The greatest concern of many beginning teachers is that they will not be able to respond appropriately to students' disruptive behavior. The conventional ("expert") advice is to have a plan that is established at the beginning of the year, explain this clearly to the students and follow it without fail. Many teachers have attended workshops at which a detailed plan for behavior management was presented as a way to end children's inappropriate or disruptive behavior. Plans for dealing with inappropriate behavior usually encompass misbehavior within limits that we think of as "normal" or ordinary. In the following case the behavior went beyond those limits and became violent. The teacher followed her plan for responding to inappropriate behavior but found that this had consequences she had not anticipated. Now she questions whether following her plan was the best thing to do under the circumstances.

River Road Academy is a small private elementary school in a rather affluent section of a middle-sized city. The school contains grades K–4; each grade has five classes with 16 children in each class. Neither the student body nor the faculty is racially or ethnically diverse and most of them come from upper middle class or "old money" families. The parents are *very* involved and the administration is supportive. Science lab is a "special" subject, i.e., a supplement to the regular classroom instruction. Each second, third and fourth grader attends Science Lab once a week. In my first year of teaching I enjoyed my job as science teacher at the school. My classroom is eclectic and fun; I stress following directions and established rules but otherwise I think that I'm not as "hard nosed" as other teachers here seem to be. I always plan lessons that will be fun as well as a learning experience.

When a class of students comes into the lab they are supposed to choose a seat on their own with full knowledge that if there is a problem or for any reason, really, I have the right to move them and that I will do it. Then they wait for their lab journals to be passed out. Usually there is no problem and the children wait quietly as this procedure is carried out without any fuss or wasted time. On this particular day, several boys were absent in the third grade class, leaving only five boys present; since there are only four seats at each table, one boy had to sit with three girls (a *horrible* fate in third grade). Instead of sitting quietly or asking for another seat, the student who was left out of the boy's table chose the smallest boy at the table and yanked his stool out from under him and then sat on it. I suppose this was to claim that seat with finality. I saw this happen and immediately walked over and asked the student to apologize to the other child, who was still lying on the floor, and then to move to another table for the rest of the lab. His response was to grunt loudly and throw the stool into the air. The stool struck me in the shin. I bit my tongue and counted to ten because I was just plain mad and knew I couldn't handle the situation as a professional adult until I calmed down. Remember, I'm a first-year teacher. When I finished counting to ten the student had moved to the other table but was not sitting down. I asked him to go to the "time out" area in my classroom immediately. He responded with a loud "Why?" I told him because he was rude to the other student, rude to me and had hit me with his stool and he could sit in "time out" until he had gained enough control to rejoin the class. He responded with a belligerent "I'm sorry I hit you" and stomped off to the time-out area. Once he was in "time out," I continued with my usual class routine. Then he began to snort, grunt, and bang his hands and stool against the walls. I let him sit there until he appeared to be calm enough to come back.

I followed usual school protocol and spoke to his homeroom teacher, who recommended that I inform both the headmaster and the guidance counselor of the incident as well as write an official discipline report, which I did. The result was a bureaucratic mess that ruined my relationship with the child's parents. Before this incident the parents had been strong supporters of the science program. The mother dropped in from time to time and they had bought and donated a lizard with a nice cage for the science laboratory. They had been very friendly to me and had given me tickets to a game, a courtesy that parents often extend to teachers here. Now they pass me by without speaking and the mother has even left the room when I entered.

Later, I learned that the child had not taken the note about the incident home to his parents as he was supposed to do. I also found out later that this student had been having a rash of angry outbursts. No one had communicated the child's history to me, and I, thinking this was a one-time or first-time offense, forgave his behavior too readily. If the guidance counselor, the teacher, the parents and I had done a better job of making each other aware of the child's problems, then the situation could have been dealt with firmly and swiftly.

Putting the child in "time out" followed my usual discipline plan, even though on reflection I feel that the level of rudeness and physical violence should have warranted immediate removal from the class and referral to the headmaster or guidance counselor (one at the time was in a meeting and the other is rarely in his office). I feel that my instinct to follow my regular plan, and go easy on the student, was totally wrong and that I really should not have let him stay in the classroom.

My advice to new teachers would be: Have a discipline plan, but throw it out the window when necessary. *Talk to the people you work with*. It's not considered gossip to give someone information that could help them better deal with a child who needs to be dealt with because everyone benefits in the end this way.

Analysis and Discussion

1. What are the issues in this case? List them and explain your understanding of each one.

2. If you were the teacher and could retrace your steps, what, if anything, would you do differently?

3. Take the child's point of view and, assuming he tried to be truthful, tell how he would explain the incident (a) to the principal, and (b) to his parents.

4. Describe what you think the other children's probable reactions were to the scene as it unfolded in the classroom.

5. Is this kind of problem more likely to happen in science class than in other classes? Explain your answer.

6. Take the parents' point of view and explain why they blamed the teacher. Assuming their point of view, propose another scenario for how they could have reacted to produce a better outcome.

7. Would you characterize this as primarily a structural problem, a political problem, a human relations problem or a conflict of values? Or a combination of these?

8. What have you learned from this case?

■ ■ ■

Case 3.2   Accentuate the Positive

This case involves a teacher who teaches sixth grade in a small town with a very diverse school population. In contrast to the last case, where a parent was overinvolved, most of the parents of the children in this teacher's class are not involved at all. As you study this case, think back over your experience in elementary school and try to recall whether you were ever in a class that seemed to have a contentious and unfriendly atmosphere.

This is my third year of teaching and my third year as a science teacher in a school where most of the students come from low- to middle-income families with a small percentage coming from high-income families. Two-thirds of the students are African-American; almost all the others are Caucasian. Parent involvement is minimal; those who are most often present at school functions are parents of students who are overall high achievers. It is often difficult to get parents of low achievers to come out even for requested conferences. I've found that sometimes you can talk with them over the phone about alternative methods for helping their children in the classroom, but it doesn't have the same benefit as talking with the parents in person.

The classes I teach usually range in size from 15 to 30 students. Sometimes I have a smaller class due to student withdrawals from the school and changing student schedules. I teach in a regular classroom setting; students come to my classroom for their science lesson. Some learning disabled students are mainstreamed into the classes. I use a variety of teaching styles and activities for the purpose of helping students with learning disabilities and to take into account the various learning styles that students have. Class activities usually consist of lectures, labs, short hands-on activities, role playing, individual projects, modeling, videos, games and tournaments. I use cooperative learning whenever it seems appropriate.

In one of the science classes I taught this past year, there seemed to be an unusual number of personality conflicts as well as buddy-buddy combinations. I always found it harder to teach this class with enthusiasm due to the fact that students always put each other down and seemed to think it appropriate and more important to socialize rather than complete assignments or pay attention. They often went into assignments blindly because they felt they didn't need to pay attention in order to understand the activity and its relevance to what we were studying. Because this behavior affected other students in the classroom, the problem was related to the whole class rather than just a group of students. Behavior of this kind presented itself on and off throughout the year.

In talking to other teachers, I learned that this group of students, which I also had during the lunch period, were basically together all day. In the afternoon, half of the group went to one language arts teacher and the other half went to another language arts teacher who teaches regular and academically gifted students. Both teachers complained about the same types of student behavior: blurting out comments across the room, name calling, putting each other down, having no motivation for learning (although they are very capable students), always looking for opportunities to pull the teacher and other students off task for the moment.

I tried to find out what other teachers who had problems with these students were doing to solve them. One used detention, while the other resorted to parent conferences, office referrals, splitting the class by making switches with the team math teacher. Splitting the class worked for the students who were not troublemakers because it basically put them with the students who really wanted to learn and created no discipline problems during math and language arts, but that left others who were causing problems. That teacher encountered more opposition than support from parents as well as continued discipline problems.

I felt that my class was a poor grouping of students because they encouraged each other to misbehave and when more than one student is misbehaving so obviously it becomes hard for the teacher to know what to do. But the grouping of students had been made and I felt I had no choice but to deal as well as I could with the situation.

Pause for Reflection:

How would you try to deal with the situation? Write your response or discuss it with other students.

To try to resolve the problem, I started looking for positive behaviors in the class. When I observed such behaviors, I reinforced them with comments such as "You were wonderful at leaving the building for lunch without disturbing the other classes today, now let's work on our noise in the lunch room. How can we lower our noise level?" I kept looking for anything positive and commenting on it, adding a suggestion about something else that needed working on.

The result was that, overall, discipline improved for me because the students noticed that I commented on a lot of good things they were doing and it appeared that most of them wanted to please me. I didn't accomplish all that I wanted to accomplish, but there was a tremendous improvement and that made learning so much easier for the students who really were concerned about their work.

From this experience, I learned that it is not only important to give positive feedback for assignments but it also works with achieving desirable behavior in the classroom. Look for positive behaviors more and reinforce them rather than trying to assert control all the time. I would try this again if I had to and look for ways of improving this strategy because I think we learn something new every day.

Analysis and Discussion

1. Consider the statement "That teacher had more opposition than support from parents." Identify and discuss some of the things that might cause parents to oppose rather than support a teacher. How can a teacher deal with parent opposition?

2. You have probably studied behaviorism in a psychology class. Outline the theoretical basis for giving positive reinforcement as a means to shape behavior. Explain some advantages and disadvantages of its use.

3. If you were this teacher, how would you try to prevent a similar problem in future years?

4. Describe the psychological rewards for students who refuse to cooperate and are disruptive in class.

5. Try role playing with a fellow student. Have one of you take the role of a student who is uncooperative, while the other takes the role of a student who wants to learn. Then argue about what is happening in class.

■ ■ ■

Case 3.3   No, I Won't!

This case provides an opportunity to consider the challenges of engaging all students in science learning. It was written by a first-year teacher who reflects on her experiences with a difficult student who refused to participate in class activities. She had planned a science activity, making birdfeeders, that she believed would be enjoyable for her students. One student, Joseph, refused to participate in designing and constructing a birdfeeder. Joseph was a constant distraction in class and his antics overshadowed positive classroom experiences the teacher might otherwise recall.

It is summer, and this is the first chance I've had to reflect on things that took place during this year—my first year of teaching. I taught fifth grade in a school located in a semi-rural area. Many of my students were brought to school by bus. For the most part, I have many positive memories of this year's class. There were also many situations that I'm not sure I dealt with in the best manner. Time and time again, my images remind me of how Joseph seemed to be the center of attention in my classroom. No matter what I did, it seemed my attention constantly spiraled dealing with Joseph's unwillingness to participate in class activities.

My mind wanders back to a particular time when I was very excited about having my students create a "winter gift" (we aren't allowed to recognize Christmas, so I refer to Christmas-time traditions as "winter-related" celebrations) to share with someone at home. I had gone to a lot of trouble to find materials and prepare them for the children to use to make simple bird feeders. I thought that making bird feeders would be an excellent way to teach technology design, and would also provide something for the students to enjoy with their families at home during the holidays. Usually I teach science in the afternoon, but to make the activity "special," and to be sure the students would have time to complete the project, I planned for work on the bird feeders to take place first on our morning schedule. While the children would work in pairs, each would have a bird feeder to take home. I had gotten wood pieces cut at a hardware store for making the bird feeders, and purchased various types of bird seed. I even prepared brown paper wrap the students could use to wrap the feeders, if they wished, to give them to someone special as a gift. On Monday morning, during our last week together before winter break, the children entered the classroom and were excited when they saw the materials I had laid out for them; everyone, that is, except Joseph.

Joseph came into the classroom pushing John, who complained that Joseph had kicked the back of his seat on the bus all the way to school that morning. When Joseph saw what I had planned for the students to do, he said: "We already have one of those (a bird feeder) at home. My grandmother put one up. It don't work. The birds never come."

I decided that he might better work alone and tried to encourage him: "Joseph, today *you* get a chance to *make* a bird feeder. The birds might like this one better than the one already in your yard. You could put this one in a different place and see if the birds like it better than your grandmother's!" Joseph walked away and mumbled over his shoulder, "I don't want to make a dumb bird feeder! I already have a bird feeder!" I let him go while I helped other students get started on designing and making their projects. Joseph went to his seat and sat down, looking straight ahead.

A few minutes later, I spoke to him without leaving the group I was helping, "Joseph, I think you will like having a bird feeder that you made all by yourself." No response. I felt at a loss. This was the planned activity for the next three days, and there wasn't really another option for him. At other times I might have insisted, but since it was close to the holiday when some children become easily distressed, I said, "I'm sorry you're not interested, Joseph. Isn't there some other science activity that you might like to do? Everyone in this class has to participate in learning. You know that's a rule we have in here."

Joseph began to rise slowly from his seat. I moved on to help other children, feeling hopeful that he was going to participate. A few moments later, I glanced up and watched as Joseph walked about the room disrupting nearly everyone on his way to pick up materials from the resource table I had set up beside my desk. As Joseph passed by others at work, he would flip over their wood pieces, or point and laugh at a group's bird feeder blueprint design they had drawn. (While I had provided wood pieces, students first had to draw a blueprint to show how they would arrange and fasten their wood pieces together using no more than 10 screws.)

I could feel my frustration rising. I paused working with a group, stood up, and caught Joseph's eye.

"It's time for you to get busy, Joseph! Either start on your feeder or tell me another plan you have for learning something this hour."

"I said, I'm NOT DOING IT!" he yelled.

"Bring your supplies over here. I didn't prepare enough materials for *me* to have a feeder for myself. Would you be willing to make one for me?" I replied as calmly as I could.

With a scowl on his face, Joseph picked up supplies and walked over to where I was working. I could see other students shrink away as he passed by their tables.

I turned back to help another student while Joseph sat behind me at his desk with the supplies. Moments later, I looked over and saw he was not doing anything.

"It's time to get started, Joseph," I said.

He replied, "I'm not making a bird feeder!"

At this point, I knew my face was growing red. Rather than argue, I decided not to push Joseph any further. I looked him straight in the eye and in a low, firm voice said, "Alright. You may *sit* there quietly."

After a few minutes, out of the corner of my eye, I saw Joseph trying to screw wood pieces together. Moments later, I heard Joseph yell, "I can't do this." He shoved the materials away from himself, and fumed, "These screws don't fit!"

By this time I was very busy helping other children. I mustered up whatever bit of patience I still had and asked Joseph, "Did you first examine your wood pieces to see how you might best put them together? If you look, you will see there are some holes in the wood edges already made for screws. You'll have to look closely and decide how you can use them to assemble your feeder. Are you screwing the screws into the holes?"

"No!" Joseph answered.

"Well, it won't work too easily if you don't use the holes; it's too hard to screw them into the wood otherwise."

Smash!

I turned to see the broken supplies, wood I had purchased with my own money, and that I had taken my weekend to have cut into pieces and drilled for the students. Now, I felt angry and disappointed. I said no more to Joseph since anything I said only seemed to fuel his belligerence. Anyway, I wasn't quite sure what to say. I felt helpless.

The other children continued to work very energetically. Soon we had to stop for math. They put away their blueprint papers and feeders in an area I had designated for storage of projects in progress, and cleaned up.

I went over to Joseph and saw that he had screwed together two pieces of broken wood. I looked at his work for a moment and tried to sound encouraging:

"Joseph, you did a good job getting these screws into the wood. Maybe you have invented something new here. What is it? What can we call this?"

"It's a thing," Joseph replied.

"What are you going to do with it?" I asked.

"Nothing. I'm going to take it home and smash it."

"Well, I'm not going to let you do that. I'll keep the pieces and see if maybe I can use them to make my own bird feeder."

"They're no good. I broke them."

I felt defeated by Joseph. I was trying hard not to let my interactions with him overshadow the experience. Nonetheless, Joseph's antics took away much of the pleasure I would have had seeing the other children work on this project.

The children took home their projects and departed for two weeks for the winter holiday break. I thought and thought about Joseph.

Pause for Reflection:

The next section tells what the teacher decided to do, and what happened as a consequence of her decision. Before you continue, pause here to discuss what options the teacher has. What would you do if you had a child like Joseph in your class?

I had actually completed a bird feeder and decided I would deliver it as a gift to Joseph's home during the break. I had a difficult time finding Joseph's home. I drove down a twisted path of dirt roads in the woods and finally located his family's trailer home. His grandmother answered the door and, after I introduced myself, welcomed me into their home. Joseph had a shocked look on his face when he saw me sitting in his living room talking with his grandmother. He slowly took a place on the floor beside his grandmother. We talked a few minutes about Joseph's performance in school, and I tried to focus on positive qualities I had noted about Joseph over the school year. His grandmother explained that she was taking care of Joseph until his mother returned—if she returned. Evidently, his mother had left without any notice last summer. She called home occasionally, but gave few details about where she was or what she was doing. I wasn't sure what to say at that point, so I invited Joseph to help me find a place to hang the bird feeder outdoors.

Once school resumed in January, Joseph made significant changes in his efforts to participate more in class activities. I'm not sure what impact the visit to his home had, but it was as if he appreciated my knowing some secret about his life outside school. He seemed eager to please me. Monday mornings and Friday afternoons always seemed to be difficult times for him, but during the school week he seemed to be much happier overall. He would try to help me in the mornings before school started to get things organized, and made efforts to participate in class activities. However, I continued to receive complaints about his obstinate behavior from his teachers in Physical Education, Art, and the Media Center, and lunch times always involved constant battles with his classmates. I know I will encounter future students like Joseph. What can I do to better understand and help students like Joseph and others that need help in my classroom?

Analysis and Discussion

This case presents a problem that you are likely to encounter at some time during your teaching career. What do you do about a child who refuses to participate in science activities? Since this case was presented by a first-year teacher, it would be helpful to have the views and ideas of an experienced teacher who can bring practical knowledge to the discussion.

Some questions for a group discussion led by an experienced instructor or teacher include:

- Was the teacher's response a constructive one?
- What alternative ways could the teacher have responded and what might have been the outcome of each?
- This child was angry. What are other causes of children's unwillingness to participate in science activities?
- To whom can you turn in a school setting to get help with a problem child?

■ ■ ■

Case 3.4   Carpet Capers: Dealing with Physical Constraints in the Classroom

This case was written by Dorothy, a teacher who has just completed graduate school and is returning to teach in a third grade classroom. Research indicates that science teaching, on average, takes place in elementary classrooms less than 40 minutes per week. Dorothy's case suggests a few reasons why elementary teachers may not be teaching science more often. The case also portrays Dorothy's persistence to teach hands-on science.

Dorothy has visions of teaching inquiry-based science using manipulatives and small learning groups. Her visions of what science learning should look like, however, are constrained by student desk designs and arrangements and by the principal who discourages activities that might damage the new carpet in the classroom.

My name is Dorothy and I'm somewhat of a new teacher. Four years ago, I was a teacher in a classroom of fifth and sixth graders where I taught for two years. What I experienced in the classroom raised many questions in my mind about teaching. I decided to attend graduate school to learn more about teaching. Since science was my favorite subject, I concentrated my master's studies in science education. I loved graduate school! It offered me an opportunity to talk with other teachers about concerns I had regarding issues such as ways children learn, assessment, and teachers' professional development. I was exposed to new ideas about teaching and learning science. Excited about these new ideas, I completed my master's degree and ventured back to teaching in the elementary school.

When the principal opened up the room to show me where I would be teaching, I looked at the furniture with a sense of disappointment: individual student desks with slanted tops, in neat rows, facing the front of the room (see Figure 3.1).

The principal proudly pointed out, "And, look, new wall-to-wall carpet! No more hard floors! Quieter classrooms too!" As I smiled at her, my images of teaching science using small learning groups, creating liquid explorations centers, and constructing indoor "ponds," began to fade in my mind. I wondered: Could I do hands-on science with this sort of furniture and carpet in my classroom?

School started and I soon appreciated the carpeted classroom—it helped minimize the noise of 27 energetic third graders. The room space was almost entirely taken up by students and their desks. I found three small tables which I positioned at one side and the to back of the room. We had two sinks and one bathroom, and a door leading to a patio area (these were wonderful resources; my previous fifth/sixth grade classroom had none of these features). I still had concerns, however, about how the furniture and carpeting might limit our hands-on science activities.

The first science unit I taught was electricity. I decided I would organize the students to work with a partner with each assigned a role. One member of the pair would have the role of "materials manager," and the other would be "principal investigator," whose role was to help their group maintain focus on the activity.

I started the unit by posing a challenge to the student groups: "Using one bulb, one battery, and one wire, I want you to find as many ways as you can to light the bulb. I'm giving you a worksheet that will help you do this. After you have tried all the ways shown on the worksheet, see if you can come up with your own arrange-

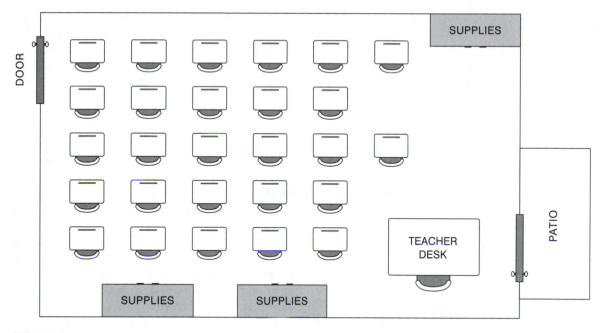

FIGURE 3.1
Layout of Dorothy's Classroom

ment. Draw a model of your arrangement on the back of your paper." Each person was given a worksheet that showed pictures of various simple circuit configurations. They were to look at each picture, predict whether or not it would work, and then set up the circuit as illustrated. If the configuration worked, they circled the picture; if not, they were to draw an "X" across the picture. Next, I described and assigned the cooperative learning tasks. The materials managers were to pick up from the "supply table" a bag of materials which contained: one light bulb, one battery, and one strip of foil (i.e., wire). The principal investigators, while waiting to receive materials, were to arrange their desks so that partners' desktops faced each other.

The pairs of students were excited as they opened up the bags. In a matter of seconds, I began to hear, "Cool! Look at our bulb! It works!" and, "Hey, let's try it this way!" At the same time, I saw and heard frustration as bulbs and batteries slid off desktops onto the floor. Groups fought over how to hold the simple circuit materials in place. One student, John, yelled at his partner, an emotionally handicapped student: "Ah gee, Detrick, it won't work because you won't hold it right! Give me all the stuff—I can work with it better than you!" Other groups expressed similar impatient outbursts: "We can't do this. It's too hard to keep the parts all together!" I immediately tried to rectify the situation by telling groups to sit on the floor. For the most part, that seemed to help avoid the avalanches of electricity materials. The transition to the floor introduced new problems. It was hard for students to keep track of materials while working on the dark blue carpet. Also, I couldn't see the students and found it hard to monitor what the groups were doing. I did, however, notice John and Detrick continuing to fight over the materials. I gave Detrick his own set of materials; like magic, the two boys began working alongside each other, comparing their work and sharing ideas to make their simple circuits work. Overall, I noticed a change of tone in students' conversations, which seemed to indicate they were having more successes hooking up the simple circuit materials, and were excited about their work! I decided we would start doing science on the carpeted floor.

The custodian who later cleaned our classroom was most unhappy about vacuuming up wires and bulbs we did not see on the carpet. I did not directly hear his complaints, but the second week into our unit, I received a note from the principal, shown in Figure 3.2.

I needed to find ways to prevent these messes!

One week later, I started a unit about matter. I introduced the topic with activities to compare and contrast liquids and solids. In the first activity, we dropped water droplets on pennies. I thought this would give me a chance to hear students' ideas about properties of liquids. As each student dropped water onto his or her penny, the water formed a unique shape on top of the coin, which I'd hoped they would see. However, the tilt of the desktop caused the water piled up on top of the penny to lean toward one side. Finally, as the weight of the water became heavy, the water's surface tension broke. Water quickly flowed over the ridge of the penny, soaked the paper towel underneath, dripped over the desk edge, and dribbled into the stu-

---

October 12

Dear Ms. MacDonald,

I want to be supportive of your approaches to teaching science. However, the custodial staff has complained several times about finding materials on the carpet that are hard to clean up. These objects can damage the vacuum cleaner. Please keep in mind that we have just put down new carpet this year and want to maintain its new appearance for as long as possible.

Your cooperation keeping the floor areas picked up will be appreciated.

Thank you.

Terry Pickett, Principal

FIGURE 3.2
The Principal's Note to the Teacher

dents' laps. All at once, I had half the class squirming and complaining about getting wet. It wasn't a major disaster, but I was foreseeing bigger problems ahead because soon we would be working with lots of other liquids—gooey, sticky, staining liquids!

Some children are able to focus on their use of materials and carefully handle them while others cannot. I especially notice that my ADD (Attention Deficit Disorder) and emotionally disabled students tend to knock materials onto the floor and become easily frustrated when materials slide around on their desktops. How can I create a workspace where my students can work easily and safely with science materials? I also need to find ways to distribute and pick up science materials to be certain items are not left on the floor once we finish science time. I wonder, what can I do to organize our science materials?

Analysis and Discussion

1. There are conflicts in values between Dorothy and the principal and also within Dorothy herself. Identify and describe them.

2. Discuss this case from three perspectives: structural, human relations and political.

3. Make a list of reasons elementary teachers are encouraged and discouraged from teaching hands-on science regularly. Identify and discuss those reasons that may challenge you to make decisions that affect how and/or when you teach science.

4. Can you suggest ways Dorothy might create workplaces and devise materials management strategies so that she can continue teaching hands-on science?

5. How would you react if you were Dorothy and received the principal's letter? Role play what you might say to the principal and to the custodian after receiving the principal's letter.

6. The teacher mentions students who have special learning needs. What problems might arise as special needs students work with hands-on science materials and in cooperative learning groups? What steps can the teacher take to support the involvement of all students in the classroom?

■ ■ ■

Case 3.5   Help! How Can I Teach Without Supplies?

Materials and equipment are to the science teacher what books are to the reading teacher; you can't teach without them. Even the most innovative teacher cannot build a science program upon paper cups and baby-food jars. This is an open-ended case study that starts with a teacher's solution to a problem and ends with another problem.

The narrator is a special science teacher in an elementary school. While her situation is different in some ways from that of a homeroom teacher who teaches science as one among many subjects, her situation is similar to that of other teachers who never have enough supplies to do everything they want to do in their classrooms.

P ine Woods Elementary School is located in a small town with a population of students mostly from middle-income families. The make-up of our population is unique due to a theological seminary located in our town. While this brings in new families, at the same time we lose students as parents complete their training and move on to new places. The turnover of students is higher than would usually be expected in a small town in this area. While we have a very active PTA, involving a few parents, a large percentage of our parents are not as involved as we would like.

As the science lab teacher, I do not have a homeroom. I work with 600 students a week teaching hands-on science. The homeroom teacher is required to be actively involved with the students while in the lab and to carry on some of the activities, and perhaps others, in the homeroom.

Our goal is to help students learn to problem-solve and to enjoy science while learning the important concepts appropriate to their ages. My teaching style is to allow students to explore and discover their own knowledge but in the lab I have definite expectations, involving safe handling of equipment, students' behavior at learning stations and problem-solving behaviors. The students keep lab notebooks for recording their data and then use these to draw their conclusions in a written form.

Since both the homeroom teacher and I are in the science lab with the students, we are able to guide students in inquiry-based learning without many discipline problems or disruptions. Classes go very smoothly and the children obviously enjoy science class.

So what is the problem? The big problem is securing enough funds for the materials and equipment that are needed in the science lab as well as for the regular classrooms. No funds are allocated for science lab materials. Although special projects can be funded throughout the school year, instructional fees are not allocated for teachers to spend money on science materials; all the instructional funds are lumped together for all subjects. Many teachers use their own money to purchase day-to-day classroom materials and supplies to enhance their teaching and make learning more enjoyable for their students.

This is an ongoing problem that all teachers face, especially the beginning teacher. Prospective teachers need to realize that not everything is provided in the real classroom as it is in the methods courses. Unless they think of creative ways to obtain funds, there will be no funds except their own to support their science program and projects.

When I found myself in this situation, I made a decision not to complain about it but to take some action myself. I have to some extent solved this problem and maintained my program by aggressively seeking outside funding through grant writing and local community support. At first I didn't know where to turn, but gradually I learned that businesses and companies in the community will provide small amounts to support school activities, including science projects. I have also turned to national companies that provide modest grants to teachers for science equipment or other needs. Through my efforts, we have received funds from our PTA and over the years we have been awarded numerous grants from other sources. This has been a challenge and not easy for me to do but I have done it because I feel strongly that an elementary science lab is an important experience for all students. Because of these additional resources I have seen our program expand; other teachers are now teaching science and their students are excited.

Success in solving one problem has led to another problem I have not yet decided how to solve, or even whether I should try to solve it. Perhaps I should leave it up to the teachers themselves.

One homeroom teacher has been very active in obtaining science supplies to use in her own room. I have encouraged this and have helped her plan activities and projects, some of which expand on things we have done in the science lab and others are different things altogether. When other teachers saw what she was doing they asked to use her ideas and borrow her materials for their students. At first she was very generous and lent her materials freely to other teachers. Soon she found that the materials were returned with some things broken or missing and with empty bottles that should have been replenished with ammonia water or vinegar or the other simple "chemicals" that were used. Now she has decided to keep her materials to herself. She feels that she put too much effort into securing the materials in the first place to let others have the benefit of her work without reciprocating. This has caused a great deal of tension among the teachers and, instead of enhancing the overall science program in the school, it has become a negative issue.

Should I intervene? If I intervene, what should I do?

Analysis and Discussion

1. Describe three options the narrator has and the probable consequences of each one. Tell which option you think is the best and explain why.

2. How can the teacher who worked to obtain materials deal with the problem without causing hard feelings among the other teachers?

3. Find out what sources of funds for science materials are available to teachers in your community and report to your classmates on (a) the sources of funds, and (b) how you obtained this information. (The best source of information may be a teacher who has received such funds.)

4

Guiding Children's Learning in Science

nstruction is a complex web of decisionmaking. It involves students, teachers, administrators, and parents as well as curriculum designers' and policymakers' beliefs about what science instruction should and should not be. Teachers are challenged at every turn. They must make important decisions about how to make science a meaningful learning experience, what materials to use to teach science, how to manage children and resources and ways to provide feedback to inform both students and themselves about the quality of science learning taking place. These are not ideas or practices that can be developed through teacher education coursework alone.

The cases in this chapter focus on problems and decisions related to science instruction. Sometimes a central problem involves several sub-problems and a teacher's decisionmaking may seem uncertain. Below the chaotic surface of the problems and decisionmaking that teachers face lie the assumptions they hold about science teaching and learning. These assumptions have tremendous impact on how teachers perceive and deal with situations. In some cases, teachers are very explicit about assumptions guiding their actions in teaching science. One teacher refers forthrightly to constructivism as she describes how she wants science to take place in her classroom. Teachers' instructional practices may be guided by a set of assumptions they have about the roles of teachers and students in science teaching and learning. For example, dealing with a problem that arises as children are designing models brings up a teacher's related concerns about assessment, cheating, managing classroom resources, and how to involve diverse learners. Sometimes, teachers are not as explicit about, or are perhaps unaware of, beliefs influencing their instructional practices. Such cases are challenges in terms of identifying central problems, proposing strategies to deal with situations, and evaluating the results of decisionmaking. Ultimately, the point we wish to highlight in the cases throughout this chapter is that teachers' decisionmaking about their instructional practices involves reflecting on many assumptions and situations. We encourage you to consider carefully the obvious and not so obvious aspects of teacher thinking that these cases present, and to take opportunities to identify and evaluate your own beliefs about teaching science to children.

Spider! Creating an Interdisciplinary Web to Support Science Inquiry

Interdisciplinary instruction has encouraged a shift from representing science as fragmented facts and process skills toward seeing connections of thought across subject areas. Interdisciplinary science teaching helps children learn in ways which more closely represent how we think in daily contexts. It also helps teachers deal with curricular demands that might otherwise prevent science, social studies and other subjects from being taught on a regular basis. In this opening case, Pat negotiates a web of decisions to support science inquiry through interdisciplinary instruction stemming from a teachable moment about spiders. As Pat's case indicates, there are challenges involved in planning for interdisciplinary science teaching.

I'm a kindergarten teacher teaching in a Pre–K through second grade school. Our school focuses on developing children's literacy, thus interdisciplinary planning is encouraged with primary emphasis on teaching reading, writing and numerical concepts and skills across the curriculum. I think it's really important that my young students have science experiences so that they can appreciate the world around them. Not all my colleagues would agree with my perspective; they rarely if ever teach science—focusing instead on teaching reading, writing and mathematics for the majority of their instructional time. I, however, look for opportunities to integrate science into our learning on a regular basis!

Recently, as part of our day-to-day routine, I had taken my kindergarten students on their mid-morning visit to the restroom. From inside the boys' restroom came squeals and shrieks of fright. Since there were classes in session around the restroom area, I immediately went to see what was causing the noise. Standing at the doorway to the boy's restroom, I asked what the problem was. Someone screamed, "There's a gigantic spider in here!" Another of the boys yelled, "It's attacking me!" I asked if I could come in and was told to hurry. The group of boys inside waved me over to look inside one of the toilet stalls. After I pushed my way past four anxious boys, I found a common house spider about the size of a quarter. The spider was trapped in a corner of the stall frightened by the stomping of a frantic five-year-old just inches away.

After the boys were calmed and our business completed, we returned to the classroom. Now I had to decide whether to proceed with the activity I had carefully planned for the day. The planned activity fitted into the instructional objectives that I was supposed to accomplish. If I didn't do it today, would I have time to fit it in later? Would I be criticized for deviating from the planned lesson that had been written in my Planning Book? All of these thoughts came into my mind but I decided to follow up on the students' fear of and curiosity about spiders.

I had noticed earlier that on our last visit to the library a couple of the children had checked out books on spiders. Because it was close to Halloween, there seemed to be a natural fascination with spiders. Several of the books contained factual information with beautiful pictures of many interesting spiders. I pulled a book from a collection in our classroom which I thought was most appropriate given the excitement over the spider. With the students now seated in a circle, I read aloud *The Eensy Weensy Spider*. After reading the story, I put up a sheet of butcher block paper and drew three columns, K, W, L for Know, Want to Know, Learned. Under the K column, we began listing what we knew about spiders. Since the children's understanding of letters, as related to words, goes only as far as the beginning letters of the words, they were not able to contribute very much to the words being listed. The rest was provided by me. After reading over our list, we were able to determine what we wanted to learn in order to understand more about spiders. Under the W column, I wrote questions the children wanted to explore about spiders. Typically, my next step in responding to the K–W–L chart is to read more books in response to the questions generated. This time, however, I wanted to involve several of our subject area centers in support of our research about spiders. As I looked at the K–W–L list, I began to wonder which questions we should try to follow up on. What would we need to support our spider explorations?

I decided that, for now, we would start by reading books about spiders that students had checked out of the library. (I pulled a few more books from my own collection to include several more about spiders as well as some "creepy crawly" books.) I had the children group themselves in pairs (I was using the Mixed-Pair-Share strategy I'd learned about last summer in our professional development institute). The pairs selected a book and found a quiet place to work. Then each child looked through the book and found something of interest and shared it with the other. One partner commented on what was said and then it was the other's turn to share their interesting idea. This was done two more times to allow children to see different books. We joined together again to begin our new list of things that had been learned during the sharing process.

During workshop time, which is free choice time to visit different centers in our classroom, many of the children chose activities that showed their interest in spiders. In the Art Center, several children used their artistic abilities to portray some of their favorite spiders on paper while others used play dough to represent their interpretations. A few children who were usually not risk takers chose the Reading Center and simply spent time looking through the spider books over and over again. After a short time, I noticed an "inclusion" child with language delay sitting with another child sharing a book. There was an enthusiastic language exchange taking place between the two students and a lot of pointing of fingers in the book they shared. A couple of the children with some writing skills went to the Writing Center to write a short story that would later be illustrated in the Art Center.

The investigation did not end that day. I pushed aside materials I'd previously set up for the "All About Me" unit I had planned to teach, and placed spider materials within the already existing centers so the children could continue their personal quests into the world of spiders. The next day, a spider similar to the one found in the boys' restroom was captured and placed in our observation aquarium for the day. Many of the children chose to simply sit and watch while others observed and then retrieved their journals to record what they saw. In the art center, some children requested black paper to make spiders. This activity quickly drew the attention of several others and soon became a dual activity. The children who were able to count to eight, and understood the one-to-one concept of objects to numbers, assumed the role of "leg counters." (I'd previously counted legs on a spider picture from the book we had read aloud together—at times it is truly rewarding to see yourself being imitated!) Those children who counted for the others would do so only if the child they were assisting counted along. These kinds of activities were incorporated into our daily center time until Halloween when we all sat down together and completed our list of what had been learned during this informal study.

As I later reflected on all that had been learned, I was keenly aware that the children had various ideas that needed to be addressed. Some children had drawn spiders with six legs, and a couple with antennae, suggesting that it was now time to learn about insects in comparison to spiders to avoid developing misconceptions about creatures they generally call "bugs." I also wanted the children to explore their attitudes toward spiders and the important role all creatures play in our world. However, it's not so easy to simply rearrange plans to build learning around my students' interests. I'm already in trouble somewhat as the other kindergarten teachers will finish their "About Me" units and I'll be the only one off track. There are various field trips, kits, and videos that have been scheduled to be used by our kindergarten teaching team during the weeks and months ahead. Things are going to be a bit disjointed in my classroom as kindergarten moves on to learning about "My Family" next month. Would it be too confusing to try to combine bug families into the "My Family" theme in November?

Analysis and Discussion

1. Define the central problem or issue in this case. Would the problem be different if Pat were a fifth grade teacher and the children had to take a state-wide science test at the end of the year?

2. What does "interdisciplinary instruction" mean to you? What strengths and weaknesses do you think might be associated with this approach to learning science?

3. Pat's case highlights various difficulties teachers encounter as they try to support interdisciplinary instruction. What problems did you note in this case?

4. Much of kindergarten learning is devoted to developing children's communication skills through mathematics, language arts, and social studies instruction. To what extent do you think science is important for learning in the early years of schooling? Give the reasons for your answer.

5. Pat is part of a teaching team and the teaching plan must therefore be agreed upon by her colleagues. It might be that no one on the kindergarten teaching team, other than Pat, feels that science is important to teach at this grade level. If you were Pat, and you felt that science was being excluded from the year-long teaching plan designed by the kindergarten teaching team, what would you do?

6. Given that children are likely to find all sorts of other interesting items throughout the school year, it might be wise to be prepared with materials to support spontaneous inquiry. What sorts of materials do you think teachers should try to keep on hand in order to be prepared for the unexpected teachable moment? In what way had Pat planned in terms of being prepared for instruction involving support for spontaneous inquiry?

7. Pat uses learning centers to support interdisciplinary instruction in her classroom. What is your description of a learning center? What guidelines would you have for designing a good science learning center? At what grade levels do you believe learning centers can be used effectively for science learning?

■ ■ ■

Case 4.2   Make Way for Tadpoles

This is another case in which a teacher was presented with a "teachable moment." Such moments offer opportunities for teachers to build on science inquiry questions children are genuinely interested to explore. The teacher in this case, Allyson, taught second grade for 10 years in a rural area of the Southwest. In this case, she is presented with a teachable moment when her students happen to find tadpoles in a puddle at school. Allyson is confronted with several dilemmas that challenge her to create ways to support science inquiry in the classroom.

Boys and girls, stay in the line behind the person in front of you," I found myself saying, each time my second graders went to music class or lunch. We had to pass a large puddle off the sidewalk where water from the air conditioner ran off the roof and collected in the grass. In this puddle were a plethora of tadpoles that one science-minded child had discovered. In the excitement of the discovery, several of the children fought to find a place at the edge so they too could sneak a peek. My first reaction was to hurriedly get everyone back on track and into music class or lunch so we wouldn't be tardy.

Disappointment was the prevailing mood and I knew each music class and lunch period would be the same. I had to think of a way to allow them to have "science" with these tadpoles. What was I thinking, taking away a perfect opportunity for life science, science in real life, and a chance at hands-on learning? Well, I was thinking like a seasoned teacher who easily gets caught up in following a schedule. We barely finished "planned" activities in the classroom before we rushed to get to our next task—music, lunch, art, etc. I always knew other teachers were waiting on us and I had to respect their schedules. By the time I'd get back to the classroom, I'd have been sidetracked several times and completely forgotten about the tadpoles and how I could "plan" them into our curriculum.

One day, after about one and a half weeks of passing by these highly interesting creatures, and being reminded to hurry, the science-minded child said, "Please let me look! I just want to see the tadpoles!" I was immediately struck by my own ignorance! I had been a member of a science collaborative all summer—exposed to all kinds of theories, innovations, experiments, and interactions with other science teachers. I was now considered the "science expert" on my campus, and, yet, I was letting this opportunity for children to learn about metamorphosis, living organisms, use of microscopes, and documentation of daily change almost slip away.

But I didn't know much about tadpoles. How was I to teach about tadpoles when I didn't know about them myself? Then I realized I'd almost slipped into another teacher pitfall, the old mode of thinking that I *alone* must solve my problem. At that point it dawned on me that this was a golden opportunity to call on Sandy, a teacher who had been leading science teacher workshops in our district. I did not let anything distract me as I headed straight to a phone to call Sandy, who was an expert in this area. She could tell me what I needed to do to gather and study the tadpoles in our classroom in a safe manner.

Although we have a Science Resource Center in our district, they were unable to help me with supplies I would need for keeping the tadpoles for an extended period of time in the classroom. Someone there was able to recommend some inexpensive supplies that I could easily buy at any discount store. I was up and running! That evening, I gathered a plastic tub and cup and went to the puddle. I scooped up water, mud and pulled grass from the area to put in the tub first. I piled landscaping pebbles in the corner so the tadpoles would have a place to crawl when they got their legs. I then carefully set the cup in the puddle to collect the live critters. I was so excited about this accomplishment! The tadpoles were all different sizes and the cup was teeming with them! I brought the tub into the classroom in preparation for the next day. I hung blue streamers in the doorway with little black tadpole forms hanging on several streamers. I also lettered a poster for the students to decorate inviting the rest of the school to come and see the tadpoles.

We were now prepared to become school tadpole experts and show off our real-life learning. The students were excited about the involvement that they had in choosing the topic of study. It was important for me to see how easily a schedule can cause

A hand lens helps children make better observations.

rigidity and how simple it was to break away for the sake of my students. Listening to the students' needs led to an exciting learning process in our classroom community.

Analysis and Discussion

1. Allyson initially felt she should get her students "back on track" to continue walking in line down the hallway. How do teachers decide when such discoveries by children are teachable moments or simply a distraction?

2. What were some problems Allyson considered as she decided whether to let her students explore tadpoles in the puddle? What conditions persuaded her decision to provide for tadpole inquiry in the classroom? Make a concept map to visualize the problems and situations that influenced her decisionmaking.

3. Allyson is regarded as a science expert on her campus. What qualities do you think Allyson has that qualify her for this label?

4. What persons or resources can teachers contact for immediate assistance with science teaching questions, or to obtain science materials? What persons are you aware of locally whom you could easily contact?

5. What reasons can you give for why teachers might become "rigid" and overlook teachable moments for science learning?

6. Metaphors can help us examine the roles of teachers who either do or do not support teachable moments. For example, the teacher who believes it is impor-

tant to be a "manager" of the classroom may make decisions that ensure that all materials are organized for science teaching in advance, children work efficiently, and all children produce the same knowledge at the end of a lesson or unit. Look over the list of Science Teacher Metaphors below and ask yourself or your group the following questions: (1) What would this metaphor look like in teaching science? (2) How would teaching that is based on this metaphor influence children's science learning? Finally, write your own metaphors that you believe best/least describe your ideal/worst role as science teacher. What situations might encourage or discourage you from taking on these various roles?

Science Teacher Metaphors

Teacher as Captain of the Ship

Teacher as Gardener

Teacher as Tour Guide

Teacher as Police Chief

Teacher as Chef

Teacher as Inventor

Teacher as House Builder

Teacher as Assembly Line Manager

Teacher as . . . ?

Case 4.3   Building Castles: Redesigning Simple Machines

This is a case from an experienced sixth grade teacher, Madeline Hobart, who wants to improve her simple machines unit design. Simple machines are typically taught as a matter of classifying simple machine types, and looking for ways they are used in daily life. Madeline wants to make this unit more interesting and uses what she has learned in a summer workshop to implement student investigations. This case lets you observe how she changes her approach to teaching simple machines and the effect it has on student learning. You will see that good science teaching requires almost constant decisionmaking.

My name is Madeline Hobart. I'm an elementary teacher with 20 years' teaching experience. The school where I teach has a student population of nearly 75% White, 15% Black, and 10% Hispanic. Most of our students come from low-income homes. At least 60% of our students are on the reduced or free lunch program. I taught grades one, three and four for fourteen years, and for the past six years have been teaching sixth-grade science. As the science teacher for my grade level, I teach five 45-minute periods of science daily and have approximately 30–35 students per class, so we have a very full room of students!

Simple machines is a topic on the sixth-grade course curriculum. The science concepts I am supposed to teach are very basic, but I have felt very weak in terms of teaching this particular topic. I've basically taught this unit by having children identify the five types of simple machines, and find out where they are used in everyday situations. Each day, I introduce a different machine and we do a simple machine hunt around the classroom. To be honest, it's fairly boring! I mean, how interesting is it to look at a screw, and then see how many different ways you can find screws used around the room? Who cares? So, my problem this year was finding a way to make the simple machines unit interesting and meaningful for my students to learn.

Pause for Reflection:

Before you read further, outline two ideas of your own for ways to make this topic interesting. You may suggest ideas for an integrated unit or for a unit that is focused only on science concepts.

My planning was based on ideas I'd gotten from attending a series of professional development workshop sessions. In these sessions, we learned about constructivist theory, brain-based learning theory, and authentic assessment. As part of these sessions, we were asked to design units that reflected these theoretical ideas. I really liked learning about these ideas! Perhaps the greatest impact they had on my thinking was in terms of assessment. Ideas about children having authentic experiences, ones they genuinely value, and assessing the different ways they learn about things radically changed my planning of units. Thus, my simple machines unit was undergoing serious re-design.

I got this notion or idea that perhaps we could use medieval castle-building as an interesting way to learn about simple machines. (This would integrate nicely with the sixth-grade history curriculum that included study of the medieval time period.) I decided to take a wide-open approach to introduce the unit and then see where the students' ideas would lead. I began by sharing pictures from a laser videodisk that showed medieval castles. This raised all sorts of questions for the students. What sorts of rooms were in a castle? How warm were castles to live in? Did they have bathtubs? How did they build castles? Were castles always made of stone? Did all castles have a torture chamber? I made arrangements to go to a local restaurant called "Medieval Times" and take as many students as were able to go. It's almost like a theme park. Diners are given a tour of the castle. They actually have a little village where you can see baskets being made by women. One man was a metal worker—he made bands that held in place the chain mail worn under armored helmets. The castle area was really incredible. The boys were particularly intrigued with the torture chamber, and they eagerly asked, "Hey Ms. Hobart, can we design things for the torture room?" I had to think about that one. They enjoyed it when everyone was finally seated in the huge Great Hall for the banquet. The king, queen, and other royal members (including a royal dog!) sat at a long table at the front of the room. It was all very dramatic. A fanfare was used to announce when waitpersons would be bringing in various parts of the meal. Musicians strolled about strumming mandolins, playing flutes, and singing to table groups. This got several of my students interested in musical instruments of the era. The students were clearly excited to be there. I could see that our original intent, to study simple machines, was quickly expanding in their minds to a grander goal—to build a castle! Hmm, I wondered, had I now created a monster problem? Would I have to limit their creative plans?

We brought back pictures from the restaurant to share in class and students checked out books to make a temporary castle-building library in our room. They found a number of terrific books, but their favorite was a Time-Life book about castles. This book was incredible. It showed cross-sections of everything inside a castle. This, and other books, gave us many ideas for designing our simple machines.

I divided students up into groups of three. Each group was responsible for researching a simple machine, finding ways it might have played an important role during medieval times, and preparing a presentation showing not only what they learned, but actually designing something to represent the use of their simple machine. I had two years' worth of medieval materials in my own teacher file, so I prepared folders that provided each group with background information about their simple machine, and about general medieval topics—the roles of knights, castles, peasants, etc. I realized, however, that since they were all working on different topics, this presented a new problem—how and on what basis would their work be evaluated?

From the workshops on assessment, I knew I wanted to be able to support unique ideas they would generate about their simple machine, and to assess their performance in producing their ideas; I did not want assessment to undermine their learning. Applying what I learned about assessment, I had the students work with me to design an assessment rubric. We decided that each group's project presentation needed to convey the following information: (1) tell about your machine, (2) describe uses of your machine, (3) make a creative presentation that will convince the class that you have really learned something significant, and (4) show the purpose the machine might serve in medieval times. Having agreed on what was expected of their learning, the students took off to work within their groups. I allotted only two weeks' time to study the simple machines unit. That meant that students had one and a half weeks to work on their group research, and then three days for class presentations.

The group studying screws was first to ask for my assistance. Having looked through the medieval resources, they called me over to their table and anxiously said to me: "We can't find anything! There aren't any screws used in castles." I asked the class if anyone had ideas for the group. Students began brainstorming "Well, they wouldn't have metal ones like we have nowadays, theirs would be made of wood, right?" "What did they use to join things together in old times?" "Wooden nails, I guess." Someone pointed out a picture from a book showing a spiral staircase, "Aren't the stairs really a screw?" That got them thinking. The group seemed content to look through books searching for other ideas, and resumed working on their own.

One decision I had to make was how to include Jay in this activity. Jay is a behaviorally and emotionally handicapped student. Most of the school day, he is out of the classroom for remedial help with math and reading, but he joins us for science to help give him a social learning opportunity. He's very hard to reach. I've not seen Jay take interest in anything all year long. I have him sit at the very front of the class so I can redirect his attention, and help him when he starts getting frustrated. Although Jay is perhaps my most inquisitive student, he just doesn't like to write, he won't keep a science notebook, and he won't do labs. If he doesn't like what we're doing, he's off flying his pen through the air like an imaginary airplane. I wondered whether he would be able to fit into a group and to stay on task without my constant monitoring. But I decided that he would be included and assigned to a group.

After the groups were organized and involved in their activities, I looked over at the lever group, the group that Jay was in. I was surprised as I watched Jay talking with his group members and working on designing something. For several days he worked intensively with his group to design a catapult. He was really into this! He could tell me how moving the centerpiece (the fulcrum) made a difference in terms of shooting small stones toward a target the students in his group had set up. I was very proud of Jay's participation, and his group as well. Even better, I could tell Jay was proud of himself and his own science learning.

On the final days of their unit work, the groups concentrated on preparing for their class presentation. I told them ways they might practice at home. Since they had very little experience presenting before large groups of people, and were conscious of how their peers looked at them, I knew they needed to have a successful presentation experience. I suggested they act out their role in the presentation in front of a mirror at home. I also suggested they do what dance troupes do—choreograph who will do what, how, where, and when.

The pulley group struggled to make their machine work. At first, they debated ways to demonstrate pulley use. They identified many ways pulleys were used in medieval times, but they were particularly fascinated with its applications in the torture chamber. They asked me if they could make torture devices. I didn't want to squelch their inventiveness and enthusiasm, but at the same time I didn't want to be seen as nurturing violent tendencies.

I dealt with the issue by asking them, "How will you demonstrate how your machine works for your class presentation?" They joked, "We'll demonstrate the guillotine on Sam!" Sam, grinning, replied: "Now, now, let's not lose our heads over this! Let's find some other ways pulleys were used!" Afterwards, the group refocused and looked for other ways pulleys were used in castles. They tried making a door to be pulled up and down over a moat. No matter what they did, however, either the string would break or the crank would stop or get "clogged up." Finally, they got help from a student's father.

He helped the group make a windlass, a bucket and pulley used to draw up water from a well. They used a cardboard box, thick twine, and a small pail. I wondered about this later. I credited the group for being resourceful and finding help, but was it right for the parent to step in and resolve their problem? Should the students have been persuaded not to seek help from their parents?

One group of girls had worked to study the wheel and axle. The girls all gathered at someone's home and, with the help of a mother, designed a "program" to hand out in class—a program you might receive at a play or conference. The program gave directions for a mini-lab they hosted. For the mini-lab, they organized everyone into small groups. Each group was given eight wooden pencils, a class science textbook, and a piece of string seven inches long. The program invited everyone to try inventing a way to move the text book. After everyone tried ways to accomplish this task, the girls brought out a huge dictionary and a concrete block. They laid the heavy cement block on top of the pencils and pushed against the block. No one thought they would be able to move these things using the pencils! The class really was surprised watching the heavy cement block glide across the table on the makeshift wheels. I heard comments such as, "Wow, using the dowels as rollers really would work!" The girls shared other pictures of wheels and axles used during medieval times including, for example, spinning wheels and wheelbarrows. We were amazed at how many ways wheels and axles were so important to the daily lives of medieval persons!

The inclined plane group also gave a very creative presentation. They created a game very similar to the television game show Jeopardy. The group selected several persons to be contestants. These persons would respond to various questions about the roles of levers (as well as other simple machines) in medieval life. The group made a buzzer out of materials used earlier in the year when we studied electricity. Prizes were given to contestants, and participants were changed so that everyone in class had a turn to play.

I felt this approach to teaching simple machines was a real success! You could tell that my students had really made great efforts to learn and to present their projects. As sixth graders, they lack confidence to present in front of others, but because they had group support, had planned their presentation, and knew their material, they had great fun doing this! The best part was that I learned a lot too! I wasn't sure I could teach this way. It was a risk for me. I was a little worried because I'm not an expert on medieval times. I also don't know how to explain the physics principles involved in how all these machines work.

Given what I know now, what would I say is important to teach in a simple machines unit? Learning about simple machines needs to go far beyond basic identification of simple machine types. Kids need to see a context for using this knowledge. In this case, knowledge of simple machines was put into the context of surviving during medieval times. I really liked the way this theme stretched my students' imaginations. In terms of the physics ideas, I think it was useful for students to notice the changes and working systems that simple machines make possible. Having these sorts of physics experiences early in school will hopefully motivate them to develop more technical scientific language, and create science experiments to test out their inventions as they continue learning more science.

Analysis and Discussion

1. Madeline had many decisions to make after her initial decision to change her approach to teaching about simple machines. List the things that required decisions and explain why you think she made the decisions she did.

2. Madeline wrote, "I wasn't sure I could teach this way. It was a risk for me." Why was this a risk?

3. What are your views on parent involvement in student's learning? Write a set of guidelines you would send in a letter to parents that expresses your perspective on parental involvement in students' work at home.

4. Assessment was a major concern for Madeline. Discuss the assessment issues raised by inquiry-based instruction or investigations of this type.

5. How would you evaluate students on this unit? Design a rubric for evaluation of this unit.

6. How do you presume Madeline's classroom is organized to facilitate students having access to materials they might need? How does a teacher prevent his or her classroom from becoming a disorganized mess?

■ ■ ■

Case 4.4   Don't Sink the Concept

One of my goals for my sixth grade, heterogeneously grouped, general science class was to encourage them to take intellectual risks. By this I mean that I wanted students to develop the intellectual courage necessary to risk explaining their thinking, to think creatively and to work independently. After several weeks of reinforcing incidences of this type of risk taking in my classroom, I began to see some progress towards this goal. While hesitant at first to share ideas that might later prove to be "wrong," students began to understand that their ideas had merit. Their increased willingness to participate in class discussions indicated to me that they understood that sharing ideas often leads to fruitful explanations, even if the original ideas were discarded along the way. Students were beginning to accept more responsibility for their lab work and for making sense of the data they had collected. I would often allow them to carry out additional experiments that their group thought was important.

However, reinforcing the notion of the importance of their ideas created a dilemma during a culminating activity on a unit on density. Prior to this culminating activity, the students had examined density through a series of learning cycles. They explored the notions of mass and volume and the relationship of mass and volume through a series of explorations and whole-group discussions. As the unit drew to a close, I was interested in having the students engage in an activity that I hoped would allow them to make some additional conceptual connections. I decided that I would read the story of Archimedes and the Golden Crown to the class.

You are probably familiar with this story. Archimedes lived around 200 B.C.E. in the ancient city of Syracuse. The king of the country ordered an elaborate new crown to be made of pure gold, but, when it arrived, he suspected the goldsmith had stolen some of the gold for himself and substituted a lighter metal for part of the gold in the crown. He sent for Archimedes and asked him to determine whether the crown was made of pure gold and to do it in such a way that the crown would not be disturbed at all.

My students were captivated by the idea that Archimedes might have been a teenager when given the challenge of determining whether or not the king's crown was pure gold. I read the story but did not read the ending, which told how Archimedes was finally able to solve the problem.

> To the teacher: The goldsmith had very cleverly substituted some other metal, probably copper, which was lighter and less expensive than gold, for some of the gold in the crown. To solve the problem, Archimedes first found the mass of the new crown. Then he found the crown's volume by submerging it in water and measuring the water displaced. Next, he found the mass and the volume of a lump of pure gold. This way, he could compare the mass/volume ratio of the crown to the mass/volume ratio of the lump of pure gold. If they were not the same, Archimedes knew the crown was not made of pure gold.

After reading the story, without revealing the ending, I gave each group of four students a clay "crown" and the following instructions:

Investigation—Density

Equipment/group

Clay crown

Other equipment—Determined by individual groups

Challenge:

1. Listen to the story of Archimedes. Can you figure out a way to tell if the crown you have been given is "pure" clay?
2. Decide within your group what procedure you will use to solve this problem.
3. Collect the data you need to determine whether or not the crown you have been given is pure clay or a mixture of clay and some other substance.

WARNING: THE KING WILL BE UNHAPPY IF YOU DESTROY OR IN ANY WAY DAMAGE THE CROWN YOU HAVE BEEN GIVEN!

Reporting:

You and your group members need to clearly communicate your procedure and findings to the rest of the class. There are chart paper, pens, overhead transparencies, poster board and construction paper available for you to use.

In constructing the crowns, I had inserted copper BBs into approximately half the crowns; the other crowns were made of pure clay. The outside appearance of the two types of crowns was the same. My students began the task immediately and with great enthusiasm. As I walked from group to group, I was gratified at the types of discussions I heard within the groups about how they could approach this task.

Most of the materials that I had anticipated the students would need were readily available to them. However, one of the groups approached me to ask for some liquid detergent. Curious, I asked them what they had planned to do. They explained to me that Joey, an extremely bright student and often the group's leader, had suggested that they immerse their crown in soapy water overnight. Then if there were impurities in the crown they would come out of the clay. As I probed the students to see where they got this notion, it was clear to me that "Joey" had convinced the group that this would happen. I also realized that they could set up a control to see whether or not this was true. However, I was hesitant about allowing them to go down this path built on a false premise.

Analysis and Discussion

1. Before you consider the teacher's dilemma, explain to a classmate how Archimedes proved that the crown was not made of pure gold.

2. There are two important values in conflict in this case. What are they?

3. Below is the dialog the teacher had with herself. First, decide how you would answer these questions. Then form a small group with other students and share your answers and ideas.

    Is it more important to let them follow through on their own ideas or should I tell them that it is not a fruitful idea? After all, the goal is for students to make some additional discoveries about the topic of density. If I allow them to pursue this dead end, I will not be accomplishing the goal of the activity. On the other hand, if I tell them it is not a fruitful idea, I will be once again limiting the opportunities for students to think for themselves by insisting that they go down the path I want them to pursue. What should I do?

    What do you think the teacher should do?

4. If you decided to divert the students from the course advocated by Joey, what would you say to the group? What would you say to Joey?

■ ■ ■

Case 4.5   Hands of Surgeons, Minds of Scientists!

Learning to teach science to young schoolchildren sometimes requires re-visiting our personal memories of being young scientists. This case was written by a kindergarten teacher who revised a unit about the Human Body. Her goal was to engage her students in a more meaningful approach to learning about their bodies. In making decisions about ways to redesign this unit, Jennifer Kennedy reflected on experiences and resources that had excited her as a child.

My name is Jennifer Kennedy. I have been teaching kindergarten for eight years. In my class, thematic lessons present hands-on experiences for five-year-old students. This year, I was required by state guidelines to teach the human body. In some ways, this topic seemed difficult. My job was to engage these young learners as firsthand observers of their own bodies. How could I make the invisible, inside parts of their bodies real to my students? How could I make the study of the human body involve more than mere identification of human body parts?

I began to research ideas through teacher books and on the internet. As I looked through materials, my memories flashed back to my own childhood experiences learning about the body. My father was an oral surgeon, so we had many texts at home that showed such things as a wisdom tooth completely wrapped around someone's lower jaw, the removal of large tumors, the repair of a deformed jaw, fixing divided nasal bones and other gruesome surgical procedures. While I remember feeling squeamish looking at the pictures, I was fascinated to realize I had many of these invisible sorts of places in my own nose, mouth, and throat! I also recalled the fun of putting on my father's headlamp and imagining what it might be like to be a tooth doctor. When Dental Week was highlighted at school, I was always a bit of an oddity in those early years. While my classmates colored and labeled the usual worksheet showing a model tooth, I was excited thinking about the wonderful real world of teeth. There was much more to teeth than the annual Dental Week activities seemed to be telling us about. I wondered, how could I make this unit about the Human Body go beyond the mundane approach of labeling body parts on a worksheet?

After about a week of thinking and looking at many resources, the planning started to come together. I decided that the Human Body unit would involve students learning about their bodies through an activity I called "doing surgery." To do surgery, we would use factual books, a life size "body map"—an outline shape of each student's body, and role play with the students acting as doctors designing and putting their body parts on their body maps.

I decided on this plan of teaching because I thought it would develop more meaningful experiences for all of my students. I also decided that I would integrate some discussion of careers into the theme because I believe we need to present a variety of careers to children at an early age in order to develop a diverse society. We started out by discussing what kinds of people work on bodies. The children created a list of medical professions. The most well-known jobs were nurse, doctor, and receptionist. After creating the list, the children discussed the relation of genders to these jobs. The children seemed to be open to the idea that people of different races or genders can work in the medical profession. Another day they read books about some of the medical professions. The students started talking and writing about what they would be when they grew up. Again, the majority related to being a nurse or doctor.

On another day, I gathered materials to begin making maps of human bodies. I explained to the students that they were going to be surgeons and create a map of the inside of their bodies. They were excited about the idea. We made paper headband lights to wear for surgery. The next day, students lay down on bulletin board paper for someone to trace their bodies. We did this with a few students during the day.

The following day, the actual surgery took place. The students were very quiet, just like in an operating room. They were careful not to step on anyone else's body. We discussed the fact that if they left out a body part, it would be difficult to live. The students used the following list of items with the specific body part: (1) brain—a black line (i.e., ditto sheet) that they colored, cut out, and glued onto their bodies, (2) face (outline)—a black line to which they added detail, cut out, and glued on top of the brain so that it could be lifted to see the brain, (3) hair—added using yarn, (4) heart—red paper drawn around one of the student's fists, cut out, and glued down, (5) lung—two baggies attached using a stapler (we discussed how staples are used during surgery), (6) arms and fingers—a black line, one line for the bones, and one for muscles, cut out and glued to each arm, (7) stomach and intestines—red yarn which was coiled and glued down, (8) legs and toes—a black line, one line for the bones, and one for muscles, cut out and glued to each leg. Each student attached computer-generated labels of body-part words to their maps.

This project took several hours. Students had to be very careful when walking around the room. There was even some surgery occurring outside in the hallway. At the end of the day, all bodies were completed and hanging in the hallway on display. As students lifted their bodies, they noticed that the paper bodies were getting very heavy from just the few body parts placed on them. Some students asked others to help with lifting due to the body weight. The students reflected on their experiences with positive attitudes. One student who wanted to be a veterinarian someday proposed that the class try surgery on a dog!

This learning experience caused me to see that pretending in science teaching can bring science closer to representing a real world experience. Sometimes we get too serious about the content we are to teach. Children are called upon to save rain forests, and rescue whales. They are expected to demonstrate their knowledge and skills on state tests administered as early as kindergarten. We forget about the powerful role imagination can serve towards inspiring learning. Our next science unit will take us to the ocean depths as divers. I'm thinking about my first experiences on the beach. What types of sand made the best sand castles? What sorts of fascinating creatures lurked in the four-inch shallow waters I was allowed to explore?

Analysis and Discussion

1. Do you think it is appropriate to use imagination in teaching science or should teachers stick to the main scientific concepts and supporting facts? Explain your answer.

2. What sorts of childhood science experiences do you recall? What factors cause you to remember some of these and forget the others?

3. What role, if any, do you think imagination plays in the work of scientists?

4. Why do you think teachers might struggle with trying to incorporate childhood science into their teaching of science?

5. Jennifer used ditto sheets (worksheets) to support the children's science learning. Are ditto sheets ever appropriate in a science classroom? List five criteria for designing worksheets to support meaningful science learning instead of being used for low-level writing or drawing tasks. When or how does a science worksheet become a science learning sheet?

■ ■ ■

Case 4.6   Haz tu Tarea (Do Your School Work)

This case, written from an observer's perspective, describes a monolingual English-speaking teacher's experience teaching science to classes that include many students who speak only Spanish.

Ann, a fifteen-year veteran teacher with a special education endorsement and experience, teaches in a large southwestern middle school with a Hispanic/African-American/Asian-American population. The experience of having non-English speaking students in regular classes is no longer encountered only in certain sections of the United States; non-English speaking students from all over the world are enrolled in schools in almost all parts of the country. Teachers and administrators do not always agree on the best way to serve these students.

In an effort to encourage and support parental involvement and to empower teachers at the local school level, the school's Local Campus Assessment Committee (LCAC) was granted decisionmaking authority in some instructional matters, including student placement. The LCAC is composed of foreign language teachers, an administrator, and two parents. In order to move monolingual Spanish-speaking students out of ESL (English as a Second Language) classes, following a reasonable period of transitional language support in instruction, the LCAC decided not to offer instruction in Spanish for science and mathematics classes. Unfortunately, the counselor's office, which is responsible for student scheduling, did not warn the regular education teachers to prepare for the influx of these ESL students. Ann, a sixth grade teacher at the middle school, was one teacher whose classroom was suddenly impacted by LCAC's change of policy.

Ann's schedule includes teaching science to gifted and talented students, regular education students, and an inclusion science class; she also teaches English as a

Second Language (ESL) classes, and works individually with special education students. Her science classes meet on alternating days for 90-minute class periods because the school is on block-scheduling. In teaching her sixth-grade science classes, Ann uses a variety of instructional strategies, including hands-on activities, cooperative learning groups, model design and building, and Socratic-type large group discussions.

One Wednesday morning, after the LCAC was granted student placement authority, 11 new monolingual students were placed in Ann's only inclusion class. Since the class already had 13 special education students, four students of average ability, and two students of above average ability, this presented a challenge. Ann teaches the class with Scott, a certified special education teacher, who is available for the whole class period. Neither Ann nor Scott speaks fluent Spanish, so Ann requested assistance from Jose, a student fluent in both Spanish and English. Ann walked over to José's seat and asked him to stand beside her, and told him, "José, whatever I ask in English, please repeat to the class in Spanish." Turning to the entire class group, she asked: "How many of you speak English? How many of you can understand spoken English? How many of you can read English? How many of you speak only Spanish? How many of you can understand spoken Spanish? How many of you can read Spanish?"

A quick assessment, based on the students' show of hands, indicated that only two of the new students could understand English and none could write in English. Ann thanked José and, though perplexed, quickly assigned every one or two Spanish-speaking students to a seat beside a bilingual student. The arrangement of conference type tables with chairs, instead of traditional desks, made this fairly easy. The problem, however, was that there were not enough bilingual students to be paired with monolingual students and neither Ann nor Scott spoke fluent Spanish. With 13 special needs special education students and 11 special needs ESL students, Ann felt quite frustrated that she had received no warning from school administration about the LCAC policy, and thus could not prepare for these students ahead of time. She tried her best to conceal her frustration as she altered her lesson plan from one of almost complete hands-on to one which had as little oral or written instruction as possible for that period.

As the students worked on their models of the layers of the earth, using their compasses, and labeling and describing each layer, Ann and Scott walked among the groups. Conversing with the new students through the student interpreters, they tried to make the new students feel welcome in this situation which was awkward for all and frightening for some of the students. As she walked about, talking with the students, Ann noticed that some of the new students were interested in the model building and eager to do their work. These students seemed to feel comfortable attempting the work as long as they were able to converse in Spanish with their student interpreter. For two of the students, being in this situation—with a teacher they didn't know, students who mostly spoke English, and the inability to understand or speak the language—struck fear in them which they were unable to conceal in their eyes and nervous fidgeting. Ann felt great empathy for them.

For many of the inclusion students, any kind of change in environment is often difficult. Many are easily distracted by normal movement and quiet talking as students go about their science work. Having 6 to 10 students conversing with their student interpreters at any given moment was almost more than some of the inclusion students could handle. As they began to engage in off-task behavior, Ann and Scott felt torn between maintaining some semblance of classroom order, paying attention to the needs of the special education students, and helping the new students feel less intimidated. This made for a VERY long 90-minute period!

Finally, the bell rang to signal the end of the period. As Alberto, one of the new students, passed through the door, he and his interpreter, Maria, stopped a moment. With her help, he conveyed the message that, "Miss, I don't want to be here. I want to go back to my old class." As soon as all the students were on their way to their elective classes, Ann immediately went to the counselor's office. Barely concealing her anger and frustration, she burst into the office of Ms. Flores, the sixth grade counselor. Ann and Ms. Flores sometimes played tennis together and had an excellent working relationship, particularly in assisting students with personal and school problems. She summoned up all the professionalism she could muster.

In as calm a voice as possible, she asked, "Why were all these new students placed in my inclusion class?" Ms. Flores apologized for not giving prior notice before the schedule changes and then went on to explain the decision the LCAC had made. She indicated that she and the Spanish teachers thought the inclusion class would be slower paced and easier for the monolingual students to keep up with their work. She didn't understand that a great amount of planning and differentiation in materials and instruction was necessary for the inclusion students to keep pace with the regular education classes.

Ann said, "You have just defeated the purpose of the inclusion class. Now the class is overburdened with students who have diverse special needs. Even with two teachers in the classroom, we can't provide the quality of instruction these students need and deserve. Particularly, since neither of us speak Spanish well enough to teach and converse in it. Even so, I know how to teach these children. I believe that if you place half of them in this class and the others in my third period class, I can provide good quality instruction and these children can learn science. I have no problem pairing them with bilingual students. My teaching style requires hands-on and cooperative learning on a daily basis except for tests."

Ms. Flores looked at the ESL students' schedules to determine when they needed to be in ESL classes for reading, language, and social studies. She indicated that it would be possible to place nearly half the students in Ann's third period class and that she would immediately change the schedules of the other half of the ESL students.

Ann often used ESL materials and techniques for inclusion students and found that many of the techniques she used for inclusion students worked as well for ESL students. With a great amount of planning, finding differentiated materials, and modifying the regular materials and curriculum, Ann was confident that she could provide valuable and challenging learning opportunities for all her students. Key factors in this teaching adventure were the bilingual student interpreters. During direct instruction and Socratic discussion, one of the student interpreters would stand beside Ann in front of the class and co-teach with her. Because Ann was careful of her choice of language used in her instruction, and also because of the carefulness with which the interpreters translated that instruction into Spanish, it turned out to be a rich learning experience for everyone involved. In addition to the content and concepts, an openness for communication was developed. There was a rather relaxed atmosphere about talking as long as it was about science, trying to understand, and trying to complete assignments. If an interpreter was unsure about a translation, he or she came to easily rely on classmates to make the correct explanation—to "get it right." As compensation for helping her teach, Ann gave the interpreters coupons for ice cream treats in the school cafeteria or for school supplies or gadgets from the school store. The students taught Ann words and phrases in Spanish which she used to question, give permissions, and direct students. As the class became more cohesive, a gentle banter and lots of laughter developed as Ann and the students learned together. Ann's favored and most frequently used line was to direct students on task, "Haz tu tarea!", which means "Do your school work!"; this phrase was interpreted as a gentler invitation for the students to participate in learning!

Most of the ESL students experienced successful learning and were able to keep pace with the rest of the class. In the mathematics classes, it was more difficult to differentiate these students and help them keep pace with the rest of their classmates. After twelve weeks of instruction in regular classes, the LCAC decided to reevaluate the students and provide science and mathematics instruction in Spanish for those students who had received ESL support for less than two years. Ann did her own evaluation. Because of the diligence and success of some of the students, she requested that six of the ESL students remain in their regular education placements for science.

By using an appropriate evaluation system and looking at a child holistically, this method of teaching would probably be successful again. An appropriate evaluation system would identify students who are close to making the transition from a foreign language to English and need only a short period of intense support. After that, they would be able to learn in an all-English environment. That environment would demand an atmosphere of support, challenge, and acceptance, and would have to be relaxed in order to allow students to learn and problem-solve together. Classrooms would be noisier than usual because students would be talking and interacting more. What might appear to some as sharing work would really be a case of the students teaching each other and learning together.

The most valuable lessons Ann learned from this experience were: (1) empowerment in the decisionmaking process; (2) synthesis and application of methods that allow a successful learning experience for her students based on inquiry-based instruction; (3) the value of differentiation and modification of curricula in a given situation; (4) the value of social construction of knowledge (her own as well as that of the students); and (5) cooperative learning experiences. Just as important was the insight gained about a culture different from her own. The experience of teaching in a language not understood by her students, trying to understand a language not well understood by herself, and trying to bridge the gap caused Ann to become more empathetic toward the students she was teaching. The richness this experience brought to the science teaching and learning situation would not likely be learned as conceptually or as emotionally any other way.

The LCAC group invited Ann to share with them her recommendations for ways to better prepare teachers to teach monolingual students. Ann stressed her belief that teachers, especially novice teachers, need an array of strategies for teaching and for managing curricula and multicultural classrooms. They need to be able to demonstrate a confidence about their own ability to teach using non-traditional methods that result in successful learning for *all* students. They also need confidence to interact with counselors, school administrators, and the foreign language teachers in a way that demonstrates their knowledge, their credibility, their concern for the students, and their willingness to work with the other professionals involved. Ann's presentation inspired the LCAC to request that the district administrative office offer professional development workshops the following school year reflecting many of Ann's recommendations.

Analysis and Discussion

1. Some people say that learning science is much like a learning a foreign language. The following passage is an example of how science learning might be perceived as a foreign language lesson. You might read the passage as a role play followed by group discussion, or write a reflective response in your journal to describe why science might be seen as "foreign language learning," and how diverse students might respond to this representation of science.

The Four Narttles of Margaflops

Margaflops are zigalots. By definition, all zigalots possess six phlumps and three hegahump catamons: jamoon, tamaron and diglamerod. Margaflops have a complex jigagittle consisting of four different narttles, each with completely different efferances and slomperond of time. Although each broops of margaflop has a different length of time in which it bubs, all have the same four narttles of jigagittle: terg, veldah, pirkle, and gilter. The average length of time that a margaflop bubs (including all four narttles) is about three roons. As gilter, most Margaflops bub around one roon's time.

2. What types of strategies are you aware of that encourage English as a Second Language or non-English speaking students to participate in science classroom learning?

3. Where could you access information to help you anticipate the diversity of students you might have in your classroom? What resources are you aware of that teachers can use to gain insights about teaching science to diverse learners?

4. Decisions are often made by persons outside teachers' classrooms that impact classroom teaching practices. What school or local committees are you aware of that make decisions related to the instruction of diverse learners? To ensure good communication, what role should teachers play and what type of relationship should teachers have with these committees? Are you aware of any policies in local schools related to the instruction of diverse learners?

■ ■ ■

Case 4.7   What's Wrong with Them?

One of the things that makes teaching interesting is that there is a new beginning each fall, a new class to learn and to teach, a class with its own personality. That each class has its own personality comes as a surprise to beginning teachers but is well known to those who are more experienced. Perhaps it would be more descriptive to say that each class has its own identity or simply is different from all others. Psychologists and sociologists have theories about group dynamics and interpersonal interactions but, as a practical matter, teachers have to accept the differences and not assume that what works with one class will work with all others. Here a teacher writes about confronting this reality in her second year of teaching.

This is what the teacher wrote in early October, five weeks after school had begun.

I teach science at a small, private K–4 elementary school and I teach every student in first through fourth grade in the school. Also, I see the same kids from one year to the next so I get to watch them develop as students and people from one year to another. I consider this to be one of the benefits of the job. In the first weeks of school, I noticed that the entire second grade was having significant difficulty moving up to third grade. Second graders only come to the science lab for thirty minutes once a week and we do much simpler concrete-thinking type activities. Third graders come to science lab for an hour each week and they do activities that require much more critical thinking than the activities of second graders, so it's a big step to go from second to third grade. The students are expected to evaluate what they do in lab and think on their own about what they have done; i.e., make up their own minds!

This entire group, with the exception of students who are new to the school this year, has had much difficulty making the jump from the concrete ideas that we worked with in second grade to the concepts that they must grasp in order to form their own opinions and do the third grade work.

For example, the first unit the third grade studies is plants. Labs that are designed to be completed in one one-hour class period have required two class periods for this group. The major problem seems to be in their making the jump from only making observations to using the observations to make potential hypotheses. In second grade I introduced the idea that an observation is something you do with your five senses, i.e., you describe how something looks, how it feels, and how it smells and sounds (but NO TASTING IN LAB!). Third graders need to go further than saying the plant leaf is green and white; they need to say the plant leaf is shaped this way and is very smooth/slippery so that might be a way that it protects itself from insect predators, i.e., making the connection between observation and potential hypothesis. I have tried modeling and hinting but they cannot make the connection/jump. They tell me the leaf is green and stinky; they think they are done and then start misbehaving. There are also significantly more students in this grade who are classified as having Attention Deficit Disorder (ADD) or other special problems and are on medication. There are also still significantly large discipline problems in this class. HELP!

Pause for Reflection:

Which problem would you address first, the misbehavior or the students' inability to go beyond making observations? What strategies would you use in order to help the students make the jump from observation to hypothesis?

(In mid-November, we went back to this teacher and asked her whether she saw a change in her third graders. We found that her outlook on this class, and her understanding of the problems the children were having, had changed somewhat. This is what she told us.)

The students are still behind last year's third graders but they're getting better at making the connection between their observations and ideas. I try consistently to model different things for them and when a child does make that jump I say to the class, "Pay close attention to this. This is what we're looking for. We're not looking for the first thing you see, to write that down. We're looking for something that takes that first observation a little bit farther." I don't know whether that's what's changing it or that as a class they are maturing, which I do see, but they are still behind the third grade students I had last year. Last year at this time the third graders had done nine labs; this class has done only five. I taught these children in second grade and now I see that my second graders this year are ahead of where these students were last year when they were second graders. So it's consistent. The impression I have is that this whole class is slower than the third graders last year. It's taken a big adjustment on my part to adapt what I think of as third grade work to a level that they can do and still have it be a challenge to them.

You have to remain flexible; I'm not using exactly what I used last year. You can't count on being able to use the same material or accomplish the same amount of learning every year. You have to adjust to the level of the kids and change your expectations of what is possible for them. So now, instead of wondering why they are different from last year's third graders, I put my energy into adjusting my own thinking and my own teaching to their level and their needs.

Analysis and Discussion

1. Explain in your own words what the teacher meant by having difficulty "making the jump from the concrete ideas that we worked with in second grade to the concepts that they must grasp in order to form their own opinions and do the third grade work."

2. What are some ways to avoid setting goals for students that are neither too high nor too low?

3. Suppose you are the parent of a student in this class with a sibling in the same class last year. How would you feel about lower expectations and less progress for the students this year?

4. In most schools a curriculum is set and has to be followed. What adjustments of all kinds are needed to follow the curriculum but have lower expectations for the students?

5. List three decisions this teacher had to make. What were the consequences and what might the consequences have been if she had decided differently?

■ ■ ■

Case 4.8   On Rembrandts, Shakespeares, and Copycats: The Art of Assessing Children's Science Learning

One of the greatest challenges teachers face is the assessment of student learning. This is an aspect of science teaching practice that requires careful observation and reflection to determine what and how children are learning science. In this case a teacher who taught first grade for 20 years provides a context for thinking about assessing hands-on science learning involving young children. This teacher's reflections about what and how her students are learning through the construction of Puff Mobiles hold implications for teachers across all grade levels. How do we assess children whose skills may be limited in terms of their writing or drawing abilities? What are we assessing when we try to document the changing ideas a child may represent in his or her learning?

I am proud to say that I've been a first grade teacher for 20 years! I have taught in two different schools. The first school where I taught was located in a very rural area of southern Georgia. Following my eighth year of teaching, our family moved and I transferred to a school located closer to our new home. I've been teaching at this school, Kerrieville Elementary, for the past 12 years. I have enjoyed teaching first graders the entire time I've been a teacher. I can't imagine teaching any other grade level! I've heard people say they would never want to teach first grade because they think the content level is "too low" or they also wouldn't enjoy having to teach the social skills needed at this age level. From my perspective, however, I enjoy the challenges of working with this age level! One aspect of teaching this age group that continues to challenge me is how to best assess what my students are learning. How do you assess their learning when they are not yet able to communicate through writing or art what they are thinking? If I try to observe their learning, what am I assessing?

Children in my classroom do a great deal of work in cooperative groups. One example of this is when we build "Puff Mobiles" as part of a thematic unit on Moving Things. The children work in small groups, sharing materials to construct their own Puff Mobiles. Puff Mobiles, sometimes called "land yachts," are raft-like constructions that have sails and rollers. Each group gets the same amount of materials to build their Puff Mobile: 1 foot of masking tape, 10 straws, 2 sheets of paper, and 4 Pep-O-Mint Lifesavers®. I tell them they are free to use these materials any way they want, but they must make "something that can roll like a car and is powered by blowing on it." I encourage the groups to first talk about what sort of design they think will best work before they actually begin taping items together.

On the second day, we sit in a large circle and each child is given one chance to blow on their group's Puff Mobile to demonstrate how far it can go. As they are blowing on their vehicle, the other children are to observe what may or may not be helpful in the construction of each Puff Mobile. Following the demonstration by a group, I allow one minute for discussion of each group's Puff Mobile. Several problems occur, however, when I try to assess children on their observations. First, some children are hesitant to speak out while others dominate the discussion. Second, I cannot have them write observations due to their limited writing skills and vocabulary. As for drawing pictures, not all children can draw like Rembrandt, thus they cannot draw objects that represent what they want to show. Alas, I find myself not being able to see what they are seeing and thinking! Not only am I challenged in terms of understanding *what* they are making sense of, but I also have a problem understanding *how* they are developing their ideas.

When I first started using the Puff Mobile activity, I used to stop after the activity of the second day, but, a few years ago, I tried using an approach I read about in a teacher magazine described as: Design-Try-Redesign. I like this approach because it gives the children an opportunity to individually show development of their ideas.

So, on Day Three, each group is given more of the same materials (paper, Lifesavers®, straws and tape) to add to or change their Puff Mobiles based on the discussion and observation from the day before. Some children make small changes while others change theirs completely, copying another group's Puff Mobile that was successful on the previous day. It's hard to know why they made these changes. Were they copied? Did they make changes based on what was hindering their Puff Mobile from moving? Did they get help from another child and not realize on their own what kinds of changes should be made?

On Day Four, the children demonstrate their Puff Mobiles once again on a track. This time two children simultaneously race their Puff Mobiles on a small race track to see how far their Puff Mobiles will go in 30 seconds. Some go farther because some children blow harder or take more powerful short breaths. It's hard for both the children and me to assess which Puff Mobile truly went further and why. On Day Five, we have more races until we find the fastest Puff Mobile, examine the design of this particular vehicle, and decide what possibly made it go so fast and so far.

I still find it hard to assess children in terms of their growth in designing moving things because I'm not sure what prior knowledge each child brought to this activity, and if they are using their prior knowledge to learn new things. How easy or difficult is it for children of this age to retain information from Day Two and apply it to Day Three in redesigning their own Puff Mobile? If they can't retain their ideas, they require much more help from the teacher as far as making decisions and changes to their design; some students simply copy their neighbor's design. Presumably, the students' levels of learning are different, but to a teacher who is uncertain what each student's level of thinking or ability may be, how do you give each child a grade?

They love this activity, but I wonder whether they are merely having fun or are actually learning something about the ways things move.

Analysis and Discussion

1. What do you see as the central issues in assessing young children's learning in science? Are the issues the same for young children as they are for older children or are there different issues that come into play at older ages?

2. List assessment strategies used in the four days of instruction involving Puff Mobiles. What can the teacher assess using these strategies? What other assessment strategies could you suggest that she try to use? What would these other strategies assess? In addition to the science concepts taught, what else would you assess with regard to student science learning in this unit?

3. Assessment can become an emotional issue when a person believes he or she has received an assessment that was unfair or biased. How can you, as a teacher, guard against assessing children unfairly?

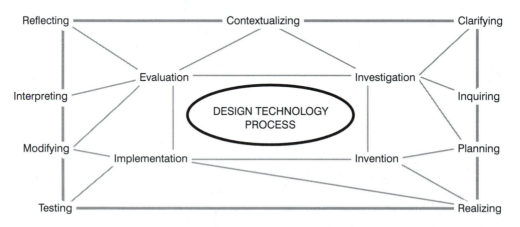

FIGURE 4.1
Design-Try-Redesign Model of Science Teaching
From: *Design Technology: Children's Engineering* by Susan Dunn and Rob Larson (1990). Bristol, PA: The Falmer Press, Taylor & Francis, Inc.

4. What is meant by "technology design" in this case? In what ways is technology design related to science?

5. The teacher used the Design-Try-Redesign model (Figure 4.1) to guide her instruction of this unit. The Design Technology Process is an interpretation of engineering principles to be used in teaching children. Compare and contrast this model with another you have studied (Learning Code, 5E, or some other) as to their applicability and usefulness in guiding children's science learning.

Case 4.9   Warming Up to Animals

New teachers often have creative images of a classroom full of interesting plants and animals. Drawings of their future classrooms may feature a fish tank surrounded by inquisitive children or perhaps a more exotic pet such as an iguana. Julie, a first grade teacher, describes her attempts to incorporate animals into science teaching and learning in her classroom. Her case not only highlights issues to consider for managing general animal maintenance but also provides insights into curricular decisionmaking.

There are many positive reasons for having animals in the classroom. I am a first grade teacher who once liked only little cats and dogs who lived outdoors. I was an avid believer that pets belonged with families who lived on farms where they could run and play in the space that a farmyard offered them. Adjusting my tolerance for the lovely creature that can survive in an indoor environment with very curious and loving first graders as well as a teacher who would truly rather not have to deal with it was a challenge.

For the first year I dabbled with the adventure and bought a goldfish for my classroom. I thought, "There, I did it!" Students who wanted to learn about the fish did research at home with their parents, cut out or drew pictures, and asked other adults for information to bring into the classroom to share. The students showed enthusiasm for two weeks. However, it seemed that we had written about the fish, read about the fish, and spent a lot of time observing the fish. There was just so much a goldfish was going to do. I began to ignore our goldfish until it was time for someone to clean the bowl. I was very aware of that need and stressed that the water had to be changed every Monday morning. The students took turns cleaning the water and feeding "George," but no one paid any attention to him because we were simply just too busy with reading, writing, and arithmetic. We certainly learned nothing else from his presence.

One day, right before Christmas vacation, I thought of a great way to give George another home. After I first asked parents for permission, we played a game of

Bingo and the winner was awarded a pet to have for their own. Whew! I could start the new year petless. I had done my duty. We had had an animal in the classroom and that was that. The other students seemed sad to see George leave, but soon they even stopped asking the child who had won George how the fish was doing.

The next year started and I felt that it was time to bring in another animal. However, I decided to prepare the students by studying about animals in general. We read books, shared information from the media coordinator, and I invited a guest speaker from the Pet House in Greenville to talk to the children and share information about pets before I would tell them that I was going to purchase an animal. After our visitor left, the students were fired up to have each kind of animal they had seen. I explained that they might be able to have all the pets they wanted at home, but they would have to discuss that issue with their parents. Then, caught up in their excitement, I told them that we might be able to have one animal in our classroom, but we would have to use all of the background information we had learned to choose the best one for our class. First, we listed certain criteria for our animal before it could qualify as a classroom choice:

- The animal must be small and remain small enough to be kept in a container.
- The animal must be quiet so it would not disturb other classes.
- The animal would have to be tame.
- The animal would need the students' commitment to love and care for it.

We then brainstormed and listed all the animals we thought would be good to have in the classroom. I divided the classroom into four cooperative groups, each of which was labeled with one of the above criteria. All of the animals we selected as possible choices were written on index cards and passed from station to station. If the pet met the criteria of the station, then the card was checked by the station group leader and passed by the messenger to the next group. If a pet card received four checks, one from each station, the pet card was put in a basket. When all the cards were completed, the students gathered into a large group and we examined each card in the basket to see if anyone felt the pet would not be a good choice. If no objections were made, the pet card was returned to the basket as a possible choice. We finally narrowed our choices to two pets, a hermit crab and a hamster. Next we had a class vote to determine the winner. Much to my dismay, the hamster won. That weekend I bought a very cute male hamster. We named our pet "Joe" and I was determined to become friends with it. After a few weeks, I actually found myself wanting a turn to pet the hairy rodent. I spent the next week, and weekend, thinking of how I could make Joe's presence a learning experience for the students across all curricular areas. As planned, I began to feel guilty about all the classes I had taught that had not had this experience. However, I consoled myself with the fact that I had to be ready for the responsibility before it could be of real benefit to our learning environment. My students learned things incidentally that I had struggled to teach them before as we integrated "Joey" (formerly known as "Joe," before the babies arrived), into our entire curriculum. I discovered how caring for a pet taught my students to look forward to assuming the responsibilities assigned to them for the week. Everyone, including myself, took turns doing everything to care for Joey.

Integration in our state curriculum guidelines was quite easy. Scientific observation and recording of animal behaviors offered a first-hand awareness of the activities and habits of Joey and her babies. The scientific observations made were graphed, measurements were made, and word problems were created and solved. These math strategies were integrated with communication strategies as information learned was used as prompts for creative story building and writing. In turn, the strengths gained in science objectives as well as communication and math objectives created and refined cooperative interactions among class members. In addition, having an animal in the classroom enhanced students' decisionmaking and problem solving skills—the skills that create higher-level thinking skills necessary for students to live productive lives and for teachers to become better teachers.

I never knew teaching and learning science could be so much fun. Most importantly, I felt that my students had learned so much more than I had ever been able to teach before because of the hands-on experiences and problem-solving skills that were necessary for their development. My suggestion—adopt an animal for your classroom!

Analysis and Discussion

1. Explore your own feelings about having animals in the classroom. Be honest with yourself. If you feel the way this teacher did at first, what will it take for you to overcome your reluctance? An open discussion with classmates will be useful.

2. Are there topics or activities in elementary science that you would be reluctant to introduce? Are you comfortable handling worms? Are you afraid of electricity? An honest discussion of these topics or areas could help you overcome your reluctance and be more confident in all areas of the elementary science curriculum.

3. The fish tank in Julie's classroom quickly lost its novel attraction as a science learning opportunity. Develop some ideas and activities for ways to make a fish tank an ongoing science inquiry center.

4. List some resources you could make available to support children's decision-making and research about adopting animals.

5. Find and present some information about adopting other animals that cannot be brought into the classroom, such as whales, sea turtles or manatees. (If you have a pupil who is allergic to animals, this might be an alternative.)

Case 4.10 We Lost the Science Fair

Each year schools request community members to serve as judges in science fairs. This case was written by a university science educator, a former teacher, who visited a local elementary school and become involved with judging class projects conducted by kindergartners. Science fairs can be important science learning opportunities for teachers and students, but they can also have some unfortunate outcomes. While most kindergartners were excited to show the results of their science project inquiries, one class presented a very unexpected response. This case provides an opportunity to reflect on the purposes of science fairs, and issues teachers might anticipate as they engage young learners in the activities associated with science fairs.

It was an early morning in February when I arrived at Pineytop Elementary to serve as a judge of their science projects. The teacher in charge of organizing the science fair that year met me at a sign-in table and give me directions for judging projects. Typically, judges are given an evaluation sheet setting out criteria for judging projects, and scoring sheets that tell them which projects they are assigned to evaluate. This year, the school not only had the traditional individual student science projects to judge, but classroom science fair projects for us to review as well. The classroom projects were a new type of entry created because few individual students had participated in the science fair in previous years. Teachers were required to develop a class science project to ensure that all students had experience doing a science experiment. Judges were asked to review 12 individual projects, then to judge the class projects for one grade level. I requested to be assigned to judge projects for kindergarten.

I finished my assigned projects in the media center, then went to visit classes on the kindergarten hallway. We had been given a particular time frame to visit the classrooms, so the kindergartners were ready and waiting when I entered to see their projects. For the most part, it was fun to talk with the class groups about their projects. I remember first entering Mrs. Jackson's room. She welcomed me, saying, "Oh, children, this is our Science Fair judge. We're going to stop reading for a moment, and tell the judge about our project." The teacher led me to a tri-fold display board which had information about their science project, and actual materials used to conduct their experiments. The class was learning about living and non-living things, so their project featured an experiment to answer the question: "What do plants need to drink in order to live?" The children had watered Philodendron plants using water, motor oil, and vinegar; some had plants that were given "nothing to drink." As I looked over their project, I asked the class questions about their procedures and results. I quickly recorded my marks, congratulated the class for conducting "such an interesting experiment," then left to visit another classroom.

I visited four other kindergarten classrooms to see their projects. All classes in some way had focused their projects around studies of living things. The class next door to Mrs. Jackson's room had also studied a variable of plant growth. Their experiments featured the effects of light—bright light, shade, various colors of light (they wrapped plants in colored cellophane), and no light. Two other classes had studied "wormeries"—jars with earthworms living in different types of soils. The last kindergarten classroom I visited was Mrs. Dougherty's room.

As I entered the classroom, Mrs. Dougherty welcomed me and introduced me to the students. "Children, this is our Science Fair judge. She's here to see our Science Fair project." The children looked up from their table groups. I heard a loud groan from the group, followed by comments of, "We lost! We lost!" One little girl quickly hid her face in her arms at her table. Needless to say, I was perplexed by these responses! With a bewildered smile, Mrs. Dougherty looked at me and invited me over to a corner to see their science fair project display.

The children had wanted to explore "Growing grass on different things." As I looked at their project, I asked the group my typical question—"So, why did you choose to study this?" A student raised her hand and told me about growing a "Chia Pet" (a pot, usually shaped like an animal, covered with a mossy surface that retains water and allows seeds embedded in the moss to grow). She told me, "We wanted to try growing grass on different things because we were surprised the Chia Pet grew without any soil." They had placed rye grass seeds on various surfaces, including: a thin layer of soil on a lunch tray, on a sheet of plastic wrap, on a sock, and on a length of plywood. The surfaces with their seeds had been placed on a table by a window that received sunlight for most of the morning. Each day, one student gently watered the seeds using a mister. For one week, the class made observations of the seeds and recorded pictures in their journals to document results. Nothing happened. Nothing grew.

The children were embarrassed about their project. To them, it was a failure and it seemed that they had "lost the Science Fair." It was very awkward standing there before the students in the moment of heavy silence. I could see they needed a good dose of encouragement, so I said, "You didn't lose! Can someone tell me one thing you learned from your experiment?" One student replied, "Well, we learned seeds can't grow on certain things." Again, there was silence. "Anything else?" I asked. The little girl with her head buried in her arms now began to sob, and there was more silence. I tried to encourage the students, "Scientists often have experiments that don't come out like they expect. We still are winners because we find out what works, and what things don't work. The only way you lose in science is when you don't try to learn anything. I'd say that this is a class of winners!" A few children showed small smiles at this point, but most continued to look quite disappointed.

The teacher showed me a new project the children had started to continue their study. The students insisted that plants must need soil in order to grow, so they were now trying to grow rye seeds on, or in, different containers filled with soil including—egg shell halves, Styrofoam cups, a couple of socks, soup cans, and, most unusual, one large boot. The teacher knew the seeds would grow without any problem in these situations (except perhaps for the boot), and hoped this might lift up the students' spirits. As I left the room, I felt sad that the children thought they had "lost." I asked myself, "Are science fairs appropriate for young children? Are there steps we can take to prevent the practices of competition associated with judging science fair projects?" I decided I would at least try to prevent these young learners from having negative feelings about their first Science Fair experience by making each teacher a banner to put up in their classroom. On the banners, I drew a large blue ribbon and printed the words: "Pineytop's Best Scientists! We Tried *and* We Learned!" I hoped this would make all the children feel like winners!

Analysis and Discussion

1. What instructional goals are served by conducting annual school science fairs? List the positive and negative aspects, both instructional and psychological, of holding science fairs in elementary schools. How can a teacher maximize the positive aspects and minimize the negative aspects?

2. What memories do you have of Science Fairs from your childhood?

3. What would you do if you were Mrs. Dougherty and saw that none of the plants in your science fair experiment were growing?

4. If you were on the science fair planning team at your school, what recommendations would you make to ensure that all students and teachers felt a sense of success about their participation in the Science Fair?

5. Who should judge children's science fair projects? What criteria are appropriate?

5

Interacting with Parents, Colleagues, and Administrators

Students preparing to become teachers naturally focus their thoughts on the children they will have in their classrooms and may forget that an important part of a teacher's job involves interactions with other adults—colleagues, administrators, guidance counselors and parents. Teacher education programs often fail to mention this aspect of the teacher's job and leave it to the neophyte to discover the importance of establishing and maintaining good working relations with all these others who are involved in children's schooling. The people with whom you will usually have the most contact will be other teachers, most of whom will be friendly and helpful but some of whom may be overwhelmed with other problems and not able to reach out to help a new-comer. The principal is mainly responsible for setting the school's ambiance or atmosphere, which is different for each school, but teachers make a difference, too. Receiving the support of colleagues and administrators makes every aspect of a teacher's job easier and more effective. It's hard to see how a teacher can be effective in the classroom without the support of these others. To underscore that point, one of the cases in this chapter describes a teacher's disappointment at being new to a school and unable to establish a rapport with her colleagues.

Having the support of your students' parents is almost as important as the support of colleagues. Many factors enter into parents' ability to provide support for their children and support for your science program. Parents may live too far away to come to school, their work schedules may not allow time for meeting with teachers, or they may have little education themselves and feel unqualified to help their children or support your efforts. There are also the parents who become too involved in the details of their children's work or believe that they are qualified to advise you on instructional matters.

The teachers in the case studies in this chapter have encountered a variety of problems, and some of them do not feel that they made the best decisions they might have made. Studying these cases, discussing them with other students and reflecting on them may stimulate your thinking about some of the issues that arise outside the classroom. All of these cases were written in the context of science teaching, but they are more generally applicable in other contexts than the cases based on instructional problems or behavior problems.

CASE
5.1

Barbara's Mother

This case involves two issues that science teachers encounter. One concerns the parent who wants special consideration for a son or daughter because the child is "not working up to potential." Parents of bright children sometimes think their children are farther ahead of other children than they actually are and forget that half the children are above average in any trait that is measured. Because their child is above average doesn't mean that the child has extraordinary intelligence; a child who is ahead of others in some areas may be average in others. The best reader in the class is often not the best science student.

The other problem raised here is that of using inquiry methods in science rather than teaching from a textbook. It is difficult for some parents to accept the idea that science can and should be more than learning facts and explanations found in textbooks. Many parents have learned science only from textbooks, if they had science at all in elementary school, and have had no experience with science taught any other way.

This is one of the cases written by a beginning teacher rather than an experienced one, giving you a chance to think about how you would react in a similar situation.

S oon after I graduated from college with a major in elementary education, I was very excited to be hired as a first-grade teacher in a growing suburb with a reputation for good schools. My mother had been a middle school science teacher for many years and I knew that teaching is hard work but that it also has many rewards. The main difference between our situations, other than experience, was that my mother had always taught in a low-income area in a small town while I was hired to teach in an affluent suburb of a large city. I had heard from my mother about parents who wanted to help their children but were poor and often poorly educated and couldn't get time off from work to come to parent conferences or school events. I looked forward to working with parents who had the time and the means to support the school's efforts.

I was assigned to teach at Hillside Elementary School, the largest elementary school in a good-sized district, built for 750 students but housing about 1150 students currently. The school is in a high-income area in one of the fastest growing towns in the state. The majority of the students are white, with about 2% African Americans and about 10% other, including Chinese, Japanese, Indian, and Vietnamese. Because of the number of students who are new to this country and speak little or no English, it has an English as a Second Language Program. The school ranks very high academically. Many of the children have parents who are well educated, with upper-level incomes and certain ambitions for their children. They expect a lot from the school and the teachers; sometimes teachers think they expect too much.

I had always been interested in science, perhaps partly because my mother was a science teacher. I had enjoyed my science courses and my science methods course when I was an undergraduate, and planned an activity-centered, inquiry-based science program for my first-grade children. Children would be encouraged to ask questions about what they observed and to think of ways they could answer their questions themselves. I knew that many of the questions children ask are beyond their ability to answer but I could explain that some questions have to be saved for later and I wanted to encourage curiosity and let the children know that all serious questions are good questions.

Since the weather was mild most of the year where I was teaching, the children were able to go outdoors to hunt for insects and to observe plants. I planned to have a unit on leaves and seeds in the fall and to build a bird feeder near one of the windows in my classroom later in the year. I had used the small amount of funds allowed for science equipment to buy small plastic boxes for holding and observing insects, hand lenses and magnets to add to those already in the room and, my most expensive purchase, a hamster and cage from a reliable pet store. (I had checked with my administrator first, of course, to find out what the rules were for animals in the classroom.) I hoped that one or more parents would help with getting a bird feeder and I was thinking of some way I might get a small tank and a few fish for the room. The activities I planned were focused mainly on observation and discussions of the insects, plants and other interesting things found on the school grounds.

One parent wanted her child to have extra special treatment in every subject because she was a highly skilled reader and her mother thought she was extremely bright. The student, whom I'll call Barbara, was already in the highest reading group where she fit in very well and was happy. Even though she was a higher reader, she was learning language skills and how to interpret what she read at the same rate as others in the group, who were also high readers. The mother was not satisfied and questioned everything I did with Barbara. She felt her daughter was not working up to her potential.

When I started the children in the inquiry-oriented science activities that I had planned, the mother became even more dissatisfied. I had not used ability grouping for science; I believe that all children can learn together as well as learn from each other. A child who is not far ahead in reading may be very good in science and, besides, I wanted the science program to be interesting and challenging and fun for everyone, including myself. I didn't want the children to feel pressured to perform but to be free to express their ideas and to learn in a relaxed way. Barbara's mother thought the children were only playing in science and that Barbara should be in a group of high achievers for science as well as for reading and math. Her mother thought science should be oriented more toward learning about things than about doing things.

My first reaction was that the parent was not being fair to me, a first-year teacher. I felt like a victim. Then I thought more about it and knew that there was a problem and that I should try to deal with it.

Pause for Reflection:

How would you approach this problem? What options would you have?

I spoke with other, more experienced first-grade teachers to get their opinions and to see whether they had any individual contracts that the child could work on. I decided to continue to teach as I had before, treating Barbara as other children were treated but giving her individual work by using contracts to provide extra work that was to be done at home and brought in for me to check and correct. I also spoke with a second-grade teacher to get ideas about what children in second grade were doing so that the work I gave Barbara would not be something she would repeat in second grade. Most of the assignments involved gathering information about topics that could be found in books at the public library—shells, rocks, insects and wildflowers. As a first-year teacher, I was already very busy and this added to my work load but I accepted it as another challenge and reminded myself that I could keep these contracts to use in future years if the problem arose again. Barbara seemed to enjoy the extra work and her mother was pleased to have the extra assignments but she still questioned me quite often about my teaching methods.

I learned a lot from this experience. Next time I think I will approach the problem a little differently. When a parent has a concern or problem with the level of expectations, I will ask what he or she hopes the child will get out of my program and together we may be able to come up with some realistic and agreed-upon goals for the child to reach.

Analysis and Discussion

1. In the end, Barbara did get special consideration, although not exactly what her mother wanted. Explain why you feel that this was or was not a good way to approach the problem.

2. What other ways could the problem have been dealt with?

3. If you had this problem, would you ask the principal for help? Why do you think the teacher did not go to her principal or other administrator?

4. Try to see this from the mother's point of view. What do you think was her motivation? What can a parent reasonably expect from a teacher?

5. Suppose your first job is in a school that has some opposition to an activity-centered, inquiry-based science program. Propose some ways that you might be

able to get parent and administrator support for the kind of science program you believe in.

■ ■ ■

Case 5.2   Tommy's Father

This case is from a teacher who has been teaching for thirty years in the same town. She is the mother of the first-year teacher who wrote the previous case. It is another case in which a parent tried to influence a teacher's judgment about a child. As you read this case, think about the similarities and differences between these two cases.

My school is located in the middle of a small town that was once a mill town, employing hundreds of workers, and the center of a rural agricultural area. Now the mills have left, farming is not as prosperous as it once was and most available jobs in the area pay low wages. The student population is approximately 60% African-American, with most of the others being Caucasian. My class is very diverse, consisting of a variety of student academic levels. My teaching style is relaxed and informal. Students enjoy my class but they understand that when it is time to be serious, Mrs. Babcock will have no nonsense.

One of the problems that I have had over the years is dealing with parents of students in my class who think their children are brighter than they really are. It's good for parents to be proud of their children and to encourage them, but they also have to be realistic. Last year there was one particular parent who also happened to be a neighbor of mine. He approached me early in the year to inform me that he expected his son to make all As in my class. My response at the time was, "I'm sure Tommy will do well."

As it turned out, Tommy was quite far from being an A student. Throughout the course of the year I worked diligently with him, doing all the things that I could think of or had read about to help him understand the lessons, keep up with the work and meet the requirements. We had tutoring sessions, extra assignments and special sessions after school. I had many conferences with the parents and with Tommy and made every effort to improve his academic standing. Despite all these efforts, his work was only good enough to earn a grade of C.

Of course the father came in to see me as soon as his son received his report card. During the conferences with the parent, I went over the test scores, gave him a list of our class objectives, a copy of our yearly course plan, copies of all our labs and activities and everything else but the kitchen sink. All of my efforts were in vain. None of this helped and I was never able to convince the parent that his son was not an A student.

I think he really knew the truth but was trying to convince me to give his son as high a grade as I would, but I stuck to my guns and gave him the grade he had earned.

I would say to prospective teachers: Do not be intimidated by parents, even if they are your neighbors or friends. Do what you think is best for the child.

Analysis and Discussion

1. What are the similarities and differences between this case and the previous one? Are the main issues the same? Does this case have an ethical component; if so, what is it?

2. Outline what you think are reasonable limits for a parent in intervening in the school life of a child.

3. You may get some insight into this case by joining with two classmates to play the roles of teacher, parent and Tommy during a conference in which the teacher explains why Tommy got a C and each participant justifies their actions and explains their feelings.

■ ■ ■

Case 5.3   Father Knows Best

Parental involvement in children's schooling is one of the most important factors in children's success in school. Teachers are criticized if they do not communicate with parents or notify them of problems, particularly if a child gets into serious trouble at school and parents have not been involved. But parent involvement, as you saw in the previous case, is not always what the teacher might wish it to be. This is a case of a parent conference that led to an unexpected, and, from the teacher's perspective, undesirable outcome. Parents and teachers do not always share the same ideas about childrearing and ways to deal with misbehavior or poor school performance. In this case, the teacher was taken by surprise and felt ill-prepared to deal with the situation.

This happened several years ago but I have not been able to forget it. I was teaching in an urban school that drew some of its students from the outer edge of the city, in sections that are similar to suburban areas; most of these students were Euro-American. The school also drew students from a housing project; most of these were African-American and from lower socioeconomic levels.

As a special science teacher I had been teaching third and fourth grade but I was reassigned to teach sixth grade, a grade I had not taught before. I was trying out a new course based on a national project that sought to take individual differences into account by allowing students to learn at their own pace. For each unit, the more able students could move through the core activities quickly and have opportunities for additional activities not required of all students; less able students worked on the required activities and, when they had completed these, the class moved on to the next unit. In order to use the program successfully, students had to be motivated and had to be able to read the text, which consisted of instructions for activities and data collection, questions to be answered about the activities and self-tests at appropriate places.

The class was organized into groups of four with students choosing their own groups. As in most elementary classrooms, the girls and boys had chosen to work within same-sex groups and the Euro-American and African-American students had chosen to separate themselves, so we had four kinds of groups—white boys, black boys, white girls, and black girls. There were no other identifiable ethnic groups.

Since most of the groups were composed of friends, there was little friction within the groups. As the groups tended to stick to themselves, there was not much friction between the different groups. The main problems were instructional problems rather than management problems. There was a continuous buzz of noise in the class but it seldom reached an unacceptable level and I was able to move about from group to group helping, encouraging or suggesting ways to attack a problem.

The daily routine was for students to collect their equipment and open their books to where they had been on the previous day and continue the activities from that point. Some groups worked conscientiously on their own, others needed help but worked as well as they could; and other groups worked very slowly with a lot of unengaged time.

One group of girls did almost no work, although they always appeared to be busy. In fact, they made a great effort to look busy without doing any work. They had almost raised this to an art form. One of the girls, whom I will call Clara, was particularly flagrant in not doing any work, to the point that I felt I could not let her continue this way. After speaking with her many times in class and having several conferences with her after school, I asked her parents to come in for a conference, with Clara present, to discuss her performance and to work out a plan that might lead to improved performance in class.

The parents, who were middle class and obviously concerned about their daughter's performance in school, became angry with her as I explained what had been happening in class. At one point the father said he had heard enough and that he would take her home and spank her. The mother said very little and did not protest. Then they rose to leave. I was so surprised that I did not know what to do or say. Finally I said that we might be able to work out something else, that a spanking was not necessarily going to persuade her to do her work but he seemed uninterested in my opinion and, after a bit, they left.

Since Clara was 12 years old and physically no longer a child but an adolescent, a spanking by her father seemed highly inappropriate to me. I never knew whether she received the spanking but her attitude remained the same and her performance improved only barely enough for her to get a passing grade.

What could I have done to prevent the outcome of that conference? Should I have called in the parents for this problem? Or should I have talked to them without Clara being present? How can a teacher know when to hold a conference with parents and when to work on the problem without involving parents?

Analysis and Discussion

1. Describe your emotional reaction to this case.

2. How would you answer each of the questions the teacher has asked?

3. What do you think were the motives behind the behaviors of each person—teacher, Clara, father, mother?

4. Imagine you are the mother at this conference. Would you have intervened?

5. What should the teacher do now? What are the human relations and political implications of your answer?

■ ■ ■

Case 5.4   Whose Bird Nest?

This is the case of a parent who behaves as if homework assignments were for parents rather than students. The counterpart of this parent is familiar to all teachers who have had their students participate in a science fair or made an assignment for students to construct something at home. In this case the parent is Emmy's mom; in many cases it's the dad who can't stand aside and watch while a son or daughter makes the inevitable mistakes that are part of learning, and that often lead to the lopsided but honest efforts that gladden the heart of a teacher.

The project described in this case has all the elements that inquiry-based science lessons are supposed to have. Students learn the meaning of a scientific concept, such as animal adaptation, by taking an example that they are all familiar with, investigating on their own to learn more about it and using their imaginations to "think like a bird" and construct a nest. In addition, the project meets one of the requirements of the National Science Education Standards (1996) that calls for students to understand and be able to solve a problem by using design principles. These principles include the ability to design a product, evaluate the product and communicate the process of design. Yet the project had an unexpected result that caused concern for the teacher, a veteran of twenty years' experience.

I teach one of two fourth-grade classes in a K–8th parochial school of over 500 students in a semi-rural area. We enroll a population of diverse economic levels, but the majority of our students come from well-educated, relatively affluent families. Most of the parents have positions connected to the regional hospital or university. Many of them would like to be involved with the school but lack the time, or feel they lack the expertise, to be of assistance in the classroom.

My class of thirty children has had varying degrees of success with a number of hands-on science activities. On the first day of school my students and I develop class rules that will enable us to stay on task and achieve our goals. Part of this is learning to work cooperatively in groups; before the children come to my class, most of them have had little or no experience with cooperative groups of any kind. Although we have teacher aides who are very helpful, they are part-time employees and not available after school or outside of class for additional training.

Part of our curriculum in life science requires that students learn about animal adaptations. Our activities range from measuring the surface area of the footprints of rabbits and hares to learning the communication dances of bees. One of the most popular projects had always been making a bird nest using natural material and species appropriate skills. The test for successful construction is that the nest has to be able to hold the weight of an egg without falling apart.

Last year we began the project, as usual, by observing the construction of nests outside our classroom and our homes. We researched the materials used and discussed the availability of resources in our area. Many students brought in nests that were blown out of trees or were retrieved by dads who had climbed ladders to reach precarious limbs. Some brought in pictures or photographs from books and magazines. When I thought the students had enough background, enthusiasm and confidence, I announced a due date one week away for bringing the completed nests to school for testing. When the big day came, we placed a plastic "egg" in each nest. Most nests held up to the test but a few did not. One of these was Emmy's. We discussed possible reasons why the nests failed, what the consequences would mean to the bird, and problem-solved to rectify the problems.

I was satisfied with the children's work on the project, but Emmy's mom was not. The next morning I got a note from her requesting a conference. I called and told her that I would be available after school that afternoon. During the conference she said that Emmy was humiliated when her nest failed in front of the class. I asked about the extent of her involvement in the project and was told that mom had helped to gather materials and construct the nest. I asked her whether they had tested the nest and she said that the nest had not been tested before Emmy brought it to school. She didn't seem to think that there was anything amiss in not testing the final product; she had just assumed it would hold an egg and she certainly didn't seem to think there would be any consequences if the nest failed. My efforts to explain that the children knew that their nests were supposed to support an egg proved fruitless and I felt discouraged at the end of the conference.

Analysis and Discussion

1. What would you do now if you were in the teacher's place? Would it matter if Emmy's mom were prominent in the community?

2. Suppose Emmy's mom wants another chance for Emmy to build a nest, would you agree to that?

3. What criteria would you use to assign a grade for this project?

4. In general, how much help, if any, should a parent give a child on a project of this kind?

5. Suggest ways that the teacher could have avoided this problem.

■ ■ ■

Case 5.5   First-Year Teacher

This case study involves my first year of teaching, at a different school than the one where I now teach. The school was a public elementary school with 750 pupils near a state university in a large city. Professors' children and children from "old money" families made up about half the school population; the other half were children bussed in from a downtown housing project whose parents had little education and low incomes. Parents from the first sector were overly involved, standing at the door looking in during the first hour or so of school each day, calling teachers at home on a nightly basis, etc. Parents from the second sector were not very involved for two main reasons: (1) many of them had not completed their educations and were not literate (they couldn't read memos sent home from school), and (2) they didn't have telephones and/or transportation to get to the school, which was over 30 minutes away.

I was hired as a first-grade teacher, but ten days into the school year my first-grade class was disbanded due to low grade-level enrollment. I was appointed to teach an existing third-grade class after the teacher of that class had been assigned a special education class. The makeup of my new class was changed before I began to teach it. Seven of the AG ("gifted") students were pulled out, leaving only two AG children in the class, both of whom were fairly serious discipline problems. To fill the seven vacant spots, seven low-performing children with discipline problems were moved into my new class. As a result of these changes, about 50% of the children had discipline problems—behaviors ranging from fighting and throwing furniture to stealing, etc. The other 50% were good, strong, average students who were fairly quiet and studious.

My school at the time was a classical magnet school, with a program intended to stress the basics. We had a traditional schedule and traditional teaching styles. The majority of the teachers had at least 20 years of experience. My principal was a dynamic rising star in the county and wanted to try to interject some integrated learning into the curriculum, which I was told upon hire that I would be involved in.

As a first-year teacher, I really can't say that I had a teaching style, but the style that was developing and that I had been trained to use was one with very high expectations aided by much positive support and guidance along the way. I expected students to be responsible for their behavior and felt that character development was as important as "book knowledge." I had a lot of creative activities going on—centers, cooperative learning groups, literature books in reading instruction, and others, but I had a decent handle on control, at least as much as was possible with this group and at this point in my career.

I was faced head-on with a situation that happens all too often to young teachers. I had a very difficult class to teach and had little to no administrative or grade level help in figuring out how I was going to do it. My teacher training obviously was very different from the way things were done in this school, and I felt that the climate at the school was oppressive and suspicious, so I didn't know who to ask for help. Teachers in our grade level did not share any lesson plans, and actually concealed from each other what they were teaching and how much they had covered in the textbooks. The administrator was equally vague and I couldn't get a good idea of what or how things were done there.

I began teaching the way I had been trained. I tried to integrate science and social studies into the language/reading/writing/math lessons and planned lessons that didn't always come from the book or worksheets. Things started to come together in the class by about November, and the children were learning and behaving better than they had been before.

At about this time, I realized that some things were going on that I had never expected, being new to the "real world" of teaching. My administrator had asked several people, including my teaching assistant, to document what I was teaching and to look at my lesson plans. She moved my classroom twice by Thanksgiving. Her first observation of my class took place during an integrated science lesson on spiders. Her only comment to me afterwards was, "You did better than I thought you would." Other disturbing things occurred. She asked me to change report card grades, on the afternoon of the day that report cards were sent home, of several children whose mothers were heavily involved in the PTA. In January, she said that a staff member had told her I was seen shaking a child in the hallway and that this incident was entered into my personnel file, even though it had never happened.

I still find it hard to talk about this year because it was such a painful experience and I know that I was without question a talented, dedicated teacher. I knew this because I was an honors graduate in college and had been told by my student teaching supervisor that not only was I one of the best teachers she had seen, but I was a "natural" at teaching as well. The experience at this school, however, was making me doubt virtually everything!! These specific events were only a few of the things that happened, but they give you the general idea.

I never actually resolved the situation, because after the first year and a half, our principal was transferred to a new school. Our new administrator and I got along great, and he asked me to show him how I was able to have such a well-managed class and to teach so well, considering the mix of children we had.

I suppose my reason for sharing such a frustrating and confusing experience is that I have seen and heard of similar things happening to many teachers when they first get out of school. Nothing in academia can prepare you for the reality of teaching in the public schools. It requires tremendous fortitude to withstand the pressures of pleasing principals, parents, and hanging on to your job. Many things that fly in the face of reason seem to be policy in some public schools, and you just have to learn to let things roll off your back and carefully pick the battles that are worth fighting. The hardest part is holding onto your self-confidence and believing in yourself.

The good news is that things do get better! I taught for five years in a public school and finally realized that the bureaucracy was not for me. I found a private school with an accelerated program and a sensible administration, and it has made all the difference in the world. I actually love teaching for the first time since I got out of college, and I am so glad to have gone into this profession. I guess the moral of my story is twofold: (1) there are many different environments in which to teach, and you have to find the right one for you, and (2) do NOT become a teacher unless you either have or feel you can develop a thick skin and inner core of strength. This is definitely not a job for wimps! It has many rewards and many drawbacks, and you need to go into this with your eyes truly open!

Analysis and Discussion

1. Point out the places in this story where the teacher had to make a decision or could have made a decision. What were the consequences of making, or not making, a decision?

2. Was the problem primarily structural, human relations, political or symbolic? Explain.

3. Suggest some out-of-school resources that you, as a first-year teacher, might turn to for help in a situation such as this.

4. How could education courses or field work better prepare preservice teachers to deal with this kind of experience?

5. What did this new teacher learn about herself? What did you learn from this case?

■ ■ ■

Case 5.6   Setting Children Up for Failure

The teacher who wrote this story has been teaching for 25 years and was chosen several years ago as the outstanding science teacher in her state. She is active in professional organizations and conducts workshops for other teachers. She has taught in middle school, junior high school and elementary school. In other words, she is a veteran teacher in every respect and one who has been recognized as an exemplary teacher.

The problem on which this case study is based occurred when she was teaching sixth-grade science. It is a story of a teacher's struggle to persuade her school administrators to treat students in a fair and ethical manner. It is not a story with a happy ending but one that presents a situation that, eventually, called for a difficult personal decision.

The writer said that she wrote this so that "a new teacher can learn that life can be rough for veteran teachers as well as first-year teachers."

M y story took place in an urban school of approximately 750 students with a student population that is economically and racially diverse. Science was designed to be an accelerated class and I taught science in a hands-on and inquiry-based manner. Students carried out investigations in cooperative groups concluding with group discussions and then full-class discussions. The problems investigated covered a wide range of both life science and physical science topics.

I had been teaching for long enough to have a pretty good idea of what the students would be interested in and capable of doing mostly on their own. Instruction was not based on a textbook where answers can be found bold-faced at the end of the chapter or the back of the book. Answers to the problems the children investigated were to be discovered by the children themselves, on their own.

Although the design of the course as I taught it was good and worked very well, there was a serious flaw in the administrative design of the science program. The only criterion for entrance was parent choice. Parents could choose, for whatever reason, to place their child in this accelerated science class even though academically the child might not be able to handle the work. In fact, the entrance requirements were basically non-existent; on the other hand, the exit criteria, that is, the criteria for success in the course, were very strict.

I believe that if you set up a program with no entrance criteria, there should not be strict exit criteria. This puts undue stress on the student and negates the objectives of the course. Students who fear for their placement in a class will not be willing to take risks that are necessary in the inquiry process. I felt that I could not create a safe learning environment for the students. Students sometimes become so worried about getting the "right" answer that their creativity is squelched. Once a student is fearful and stressed, parents often pressure the teacher to reduce the requirements or give higher grades on the student's work. Now the student, the parent, and the teacher are stressed. This is not the ideal situation for what should be an exciting experience.

This was an ongoing problem with serious repercussions at the end of each grading period. If a student had a C average by mid-year, he or she was removed from the program. Students who were cut from the class at mid-year were made to feel like failures because they got a C. In an accelerated course a C is quite acceptable, especially when there were no entrance criteria for the course and some of the students were not the academically strongest or ablest ones in the school. Receiving a grade of C and having to change to the "regular" class at mid-year was devastating for some students' self esteem. It's easy to imagine how a student would feel. It was also devastating for me to do that to a student. The catch-22 situation for me was to maintain the "acceleratedness" of the course and not let anyone get below a B. When you have some low-average students in an accelerated course, that becomes very difficult.

The first thing I did was contact the people in the central office who set up the program to try to get them to change the program at one end or the other—either develop criteria for entrance into the program or eliminate the exit criteria. Neither idea was acceptable to the administration. The administration's argument against a strict academic set of entrance criteria was partially based upon racial balance; by not having having an academic basis for entrance, an acceptable balance could be maintained. Alternately, I pushed for the same type of inquiry program for all science classes. I was told that this type of class would not work with lower ability students. (I knew that this wasn't true because I had taught this way to general level ninth graders and it worked just fine.)

I'm sorry to say that my efforts met with no success. The accelerated program still exists and the students who stay in the program but get a B are advised to take the physical science course again when they go to high school. Now students are convinced that if they don't get an A, they are failures. This is reminiscent of the No Fear t-shirt slogan, "Second place is the first loser." This attitude is personally unacceptable to me. It is equally unacceptable to me to give a student an A that is unearned.

My decision, after many years of attempting to change things, was to leave the school and find another position. I learned a great deal from this experience. If one thing doesn't work, try something else. Persevere! If the situation is impossible, don't make yourself sick over it. There are other people who will value your experience.

Analysis and Discussion

1. Describe or characterize the teacher's dilemma. What does this tell you about the teacher's values?

2. Explain what the teacher meant by "entrance criteria" and "exit criteria." What would you suggest as suitable entrance criteria for an accelerated class?

3. What are some of the assumptions about (a) teaching, and (b) learning that underlie having an "accelerated" class for sixth-grade students? What is your personal feeling about having an accelerated class at this grade level?

4. List and explain some of the characteristics of a "safe learning environment." What makes a learning environment safe for you as a learner?

5. Do you think it was a "cop out" for the teacher to leave? Not everyone can leave one job and seek another. Could there have been another solution?

■ ■ ■

Case 5.7   Science Partners and Uncertain Liaisons

Classroom teachers are encouraged to develop partnerships with local community agencies. In this unresolved case, Jamie, a fourth-grade teacher, has agreed to let undergraduate science majors from a local university visit her classroom weekly to conduct hands-on science activities. While the science activities are exciting, there are problems associated with the activities the visitors are presenting to her students. Jamie wonders how she should approach the science partners and what she should tell them about their science teaching roles in her classroom.

I'm Jamie, a fourth-grade teacher. I teach in a school located near a large university that is well-known for being a science research institution. With several Nobel Prize Laureates in their midst, the university is proud to offer science resources to local schools. Undergraduate volunteers from the university's College of Science visit our school once a week, bringing interesting science experiments to our classrooms. Problems occur, however, as these well-intended visitors don't always convey appropriate teaching practices or concepts to our students.

We often refer to the university science volunteers as "the science guys." The science guys typically visit in teams of two or three, and there is at least one female in the group. My students look forward to their visits as they often perform impressive science demonstrations. We've seen awesome demonstrations such as a Van de Graff generator that makes students' hair stand up, and a banana that shattered like glass after being placed in liquid nitrogen.

During the science guys' last visit, however, I felt awkward about what took place. As usual, I had no idea what the science guys were going to do; their activities are not necessarily connected to topics I am teaching. The science guys, chemistry undergraduate students, one female and one male, gathered my students around a table in the center of our classroom. For the first 20 minutes, the science guys discussed and shared pictures about volcanoes. As a climactic event, they set up a model volcano. The volcano was made using a cup of baking soda placed under a dome of cardboard with playdough molded on top to look like a volcano. A student was invited to pour vinegar into a hole at the top of the volcano. The children squealed with delight as pink fluid bubbled forth over the edges of the volcano's caldera!

One of the science guys shifted the discussion to talk about "volatile gases." He asked me to turn out the classroom lights and then told the children to sit back away from the table to avoid getting anything spilled on them. I watched as he poured fluid onto the table top, then touched a lighted match to the table surface. Poof! The students "oohed" and "aahed" as fire quickly rose up, then went out. He did this again, making a "flaming fraction" by pouring alcohol to cover half of the table. (My students hadn't studied fractions yet this year, but the flaming activity excited them all the same!) The students cheered and asked to see the flaming fraction again.

Pause for Reflection:

What would you do now if you were the teacher?

I quickly turned on the lights, stepped forward and announced that the science guys' time was over. Fortunately, the time really had gotten quite late. The science visitors brought the activity to a close and rapidly left. There was no time to say anything to them as we were late for lunch.

I'm not sure what to do about these science partners. Since I'm very busy, it's hard to determine in advance the plans of every team coming into my classroom to demonstrate. (I also have prospective teachers coming into my class to teach science lessons.) What can I do to make sure the activities of visiting partners are appropriate for our classroom? Not only am I worried about safety, but how can I encourage visitors to link their activities to lessons I am teaching?

A scientist gives a classroom demonstration.

Analysis and Discussion

1. This case presents structural, human relations and political issues. Identify and describe each of them.

2. If you were responsible for designing a handout that presents safety guidelines for teachers and visitors to follow for teaching science in classrooms, what would you write on this handout?

3. What kinds of science partnerships might be helpful for teachers to establish within their local communities?

4. What are some pros and cons of creating science partnerships with community agencies?

5. Imagine that you are on the school's Partnerships Committee. Jamie has come to a Committee meeting to share her case and to ask for advice. She is frustrated because the flaming fractions incident, in addition to being very dangerous, actually damaged the table top, and the school will need to purchase a new table for her classroom. More importantly, she does not feel time is well used during the science guys' visit since their activities do not always relate to concepts she is teaching. Jamie also knows that other teachers perceive this same problem. What would you advise her to do as an immediate response? What long-term steps would you advise be taken to ensure that partnerships play a valued role in teachers' classrooms?

6

Writing Cases from Your Own Experience

The cases in the previous chapters are stories taken from teachers' own experiences. These cases were not based on theoretical positions or on established practice in a field but given as examples of the kinds of problems and dilemmas encountered over and over in the daily lives of teachers. They were written to become the basis for reflection and discussion, leading to greater understanding of teaching as an enterprise that requires much more than content knowledge.

Learning from case studies occurs in two ways—responding to cases written by others and writing them yourself. Although the cases in this book were written for the benefit of the reader, not the writer, the process of selecting an incident, isolating the incident from its surroundings, reflecting on it and composing a story can be as useful to the writer as to those who read and study it. The purpose of this chapter is to help you learn to write cases, and to persuade you to do so, as a means of your own professional growth. Whether you are a prospective teacher engaged in a practicum or internship or a beginning, or even experienced, teacher, writing a case can be a powerful learning experience.

Day to Day in the Science Classroom

Activity-centered science classrooms are very busy places. When all goes well, children are engaged in learning activities that interest them; their interactions are friendly, or at least civil; no one gets hurt; the activities work out as planned; and the teacher can move from group to group, asking questions, answering questions and helping as needed. The cases you have read in this book have shown that things do not always go the way they should; many different kinds of problems can, and do, arise and the teacher can be pulled in many directions. Even if everything goes as planned, the teacher is still pulled in many directions because of the nature of children and of the activities in which they are engaged.

When one child misbehaves, the others do not sit silently waiting for the problem to be resolved. When a science lesson does not go as planned and the teacher tries to salvage what she can of the lesson, some of the children find other uses for the materials prepared for the lesson. When there is conflict with a parent or colleague, the teacher cannot take a day off to think about it or try to get help; lesson preparation and the daily life in the classroom continue without pause.

How can a teacher make sense of all of this? What can one do to prevent the feeling of lurching from day to day, always feeling harried and out of time? How does one make meaning for oneself and help the children make meaning for themselves from their experiences in the science classroom? In addressing similar questions, Wasserman (1993) wrote:

> In learning to apply knowledge to practice, we need to go beyond what we see and hear, to draw out understanding in and around what is happening. Applying knowledge

involves more than merely adding up the pieces of what is seen and heard. It requires that we make meaning from experience, to figure out "What does this mean?" (p. 11)

Making Meaning Through Case Writing

In going beyond what we see and hear, we continuously, and usually unconsciously, attribute meaning to things and to the actions of other people. What does it mean when a child is defiant? What does it mean when a parent questions everything a teacher does or, on the other hand, never has any contact at all with the teacher, either in writing or in person? People do not respond only to "objective reality," as seen by an outside observer, but to how they themselves perceive and interpret interactions with other people and situations. Writing and studying your own cases is one way to look at, and thus become aware of, your own perceptions and interpretations of events that affect you directly. McLaughlin, Talbert and Bascia (1990) point out that "[e]ffective teaching depends on . . . how teachers think and feel about what they do" (p. 3), but teachers must first become aware of how they think and feel.

One way to find meaning in whatever you do, including teaching science, is to organize your thoughts and then write about your experiences. Have you ever started to write about an incident or event in your life or about your feelings and found that the act of writing forced you to think differently about the incident or to clarify your feelings? Perhaps you had to organize your thoughts or found that you weren't sure of exactly what happened or what you thought until you started to write it down. The meaning of the event became clearer as you reflected on it or you found that you weren't sure how you felt until you had to put it into words. "You know what I mean?" is a useful question in conversation where intonation and facial expression carry meaning but it doesn't make sense in a letter or a memo. You have to write what you mean and, in order to do that, you first have to be clear in your own mind.

Reflecting on Experience

Writing cases is in some ways like keeping a journal; it encourages reflection and the development of the ability to take a critical look at oneself. Writing your own cases can help you understand some of the things that have puzzled or concerned you; to see where you might have made a better decision or to confirm the appropriateness of your action taken in haste. Your own cases can then be the basis of discussion with colleagues who are also seeking to make meaning of their experiences in order to become more effective teachers of science.

Writing about an event or your feelings also forces you to be selective. You can't write every detail of an event unless you want the reader to be terminally bored and the same is true of writing about your feelings. A few famous novelists have written entire books about one day in someone's life but even those are full of reflections of past times and events. The writer must choose what is most important, what must be included, and what can be left out.

Think back to the cases in this book and the process that the teacher went through as each case was written. Each step in the process required thought and imagination. Each teacher who wrote a case had to choose one thing, from among many possibilities, to serve as the basis for constructive discussion and be instructive for others, and isolate it from all that was happening at the same time, both in the classroom and in the teacher's mind.

Writing honestly about events in which we have played a part always involves some risk, particularly when the writing is shared with others, but growth always involves some risk. "Nothing ventured, nothing gained" applies not only to our professional lives, but to other aspects of our lives as well. Writing is always a creative act. To write about an event is to re-create it and in the re-creation we see and understand the event and ourselves in ways that we were not able to see or understand at the time. Teachers who never look back on events and their responses to them have no means of learning from their mistakes—or their successes—and have no way to move beyond their initial level of competence. In relating an exchange between a student teacher and an experienced teacher, Wasserman (1993) had this to say about risk in teaching:

> Risk is in the eye of the beholder. I think it's more risky to be stagnant, to do the same things day after day, year after year, to bore kids to death and to mummify yourself. I much prefer to take the risks that allow you to challenge yourself, to do what's required to grow on the job. You can't have growth without risk. And who wants a teacher who's not willing to take the risks to grow? . . . [be] unafraid to be who you are, unafraid to be open to looking at yourself, to growing on the job. (p. 205)

The following sections are for those who choose to try case writing as a means for professional growth.

Choosing a Case from Teaching Science

Writing a case from your experience in teaching science begins by selecting what you will write about. The choices are more limited for students in practicum or field placements but anyone who spends even a day in a classroom sees or experiences moments when a teacher must make a quick decision or learns of ongoing situations that pose dilemmas for the teacher. Some of these are forgotten in the tumult of the day's events, but others linger in memory and form the pool of incidents or situations from which cases are chosen.

One way to get started is to think back over the past week and recall incidents that occurred during a science class that you felt uneasy about, that remain unresolved or that were resolved in a way that was not satisfactory to you. Many of the case studies in chapters 3 and 4 were based on incidents of this kind. Here are some questions that may help you select the raw material for a case:

■ Was there a moment during science class when you had to make a decision about a child's behavior without as much time or information as you would have liked to have had? Could it have happened in any class or was it specific to science? What led up to the incident? What were the consequences of your decision?

- Did you teach a science lesson that failed? Why did that happen? Was it because you didn't plan well enough? If so, what part of the planning was insufficient? Or was the activity inappropriate for the age group or grade level, either too difficult or too simple?

- Did you have to scrap a plan for a science lesson you worked hard on and really liked? Did the alternative lesson turn out as well as you would have wished?

- As an intern or student teacher, did you misunderstand a task assigned to you by the supervising teacher? How did you react? How did she or he react? How was this related to your teaching of science?

Incidents, as those suggested above, are one source of cases. Another source are situations or relationships that pose an ongoing problem. This may include your interactions with a child, a parent or an administrator, or relationships between children themselves that are producing tension or hard feelings. Many of the cases in chapter 5 are of this type. Here are some questions that may stimulate your thinking:

- Is there one child or a small group of children who seem hostile and uncooperative during science class? Under what circumstances has this behavior occurred? What have you done to address the situation?

- As an intern or student teacher, do you feel tension between yourself and your supervising teacher over the way you want to teach science? How does this manifest itself? Has the tension occurred over all your science lessons? How has this been addressed by either of you?

- Are there parents who have expressed disapproval of activity-centered science teaching? Does the administration expect you to maintain a classroom that is always quiet and orderly? How have you approached this ongoing source of frustration?

Useful guidelines for writing a case can also be found in Shulman and Mesa-Bains (1993).

When you have made a tentative selection, the following criteria may help you decide whether the incident or the situation is suitable and whether further effort will be rewarded. If one or more of these are present, the case may reward the effort required to continue.

- It is specific to science teaching rather than a general problem.
- It had or continues to have an emotional impact. You can't get it out of your mind.
- You feel uncertain or unsatisfied with your decision. The outcome was not what you wanted.
- Each solution has a drawback; there is really no right or wrong solution, although one may be better than others.
- It is the kind of problem that occurs over and over again.
- There are ethical or moral implications that need to be worked through.

■ Writing the Case

Some people write more freely and easily when they are alone; writing a case in this way is similar to writing in a journal. Others are stimulated by discussing ideas in a group. Some of the case studies in this book are based on cases written by teachers working alone and others are based on cases written by teachers in workshops. In the latter, a small group of teachers, led by a science educator, discussed barriers to successful science teaching and the problems and dilemmas encountered in their work. After a period of discussion and exchange of ideas, computers were made available and each teacher used the protocol in Figure 6.1 to write a case. A similar procedure or process could be used by a small group of students or colleagues who get together on their own, with or without a more experienced person as facilitator, to write cases and then share and discuss them. Whether you are working alone or in a group, the protocol in Figure 6.1 may be a useful guide.

After you have written the case, it is a good idea to set it aside for a day or two and then come back to it with a fresh outlook. After rereading and editing, you are ready for the next step. There are many aspects to learning from writing cases. First is the writing itself. To write about something is to think of it in a new way and to understand it better. Next is the examination and analysis, the attempt to make meaning from the experience. The questions below will be helpful as you seek to go beyond *what* happened and try to understand *why* it happened as it did.

- ■ What were your feelings as the incident was taking place? What are your feelings about it now?
- ■ Were your values at stake? Were your values in conflict with another person's values?
- ■ What motives do you ascribe to yourself? To each of the other people involved? Are you justified in ascribing these motives?
- ■ If you had it to do over again, how would you act differently? If the situation is ongoing, what are your options in trying to resolve it?
- ■ Did you assign blame to one of those involved? Is there another way to look at what happened? Can you talk to the person you believe was at fault to bring closure to the incident?

The last part of the process is to discuss your case with colleagues. To be useful, discussion should focus on questions that touch on the heart of the problem or the dilemma. All participants should have time to study the case and give their own interpretations of what happened, why it happened and what meaning it has for each discussant. Through this process, the participants may each learn something surprising about themselves. Because there is risk in exposing one's mistakes, miscalculations, less-than-ideal relationships and ethical dilemmas, there has to be trust among all the participants.

The example below illustrates the three steps of selecting, writing and discussing a case from one's own experience.

PROTOCOL FOR CASE WRITING

**Exploration of Barriers to Teaching Activity-Centered Science —
and How to Overcome Them**

Cases are useful for capturing interesting science teaching adventures and dilemmas. In writing your own case, you will use a real classroom situation to describe a personal science teaching experience. The case will be more vivid and interesting if you include as many details as you can remember. Your case may include any or all of the following components.

Case Components

Setting

Describe your school — size, location, student population (diverse? middle
　　income, low income?) parents (involved, uninvolved?) and so on.
Your class — level, size, special characteristics
Help the reader "see" your school and your class
Describe your teaching style (a "tight ship," relaxed, etc.)

The Problem/Barrier/Challenge

Describe the problem or barrier. Was it related to a whole class, a group, one child,
　　a parent, an administrator?
What else was happening at the same time?
Was it an ongoing problem or a one-time incident?
Why did this challenge/trouble you?

Your Action/Reaction

Describe what you did to solve/resolve the problem.
What were you thinking?
Did you turn to anyone else for help? If so, to whom?

The Outcome: Closed or Open

Is your case closed (has been resolved) or open (does not yet have closure)?
What was the outcome/result of your actions?
Was it what you hoped it would be? Are you satisfied?
Would you treat the problem the same way again? Why or why not?

FIGURE 6.1
Protocol for Case Writing

■ Sandra D'Angelo's Case: An Example

Sandra is a fourth-grade teacher who is supervising Michelle Lundquist, a student teacher. Sandra enjoys teaching science and her students look forward to science class three afternoons a week. The students have been excited to have Michelle as another teacher in the classroom. Sandra has joined a group of teachers who meet twice a month in the evening to discuss their work in an atmosphere that does not have all the pressures that are present during the school day. They have found that it is almost impossible to have a serious discussion with another teacher at school during the day.

After a problem arose in Sandra's class last week, she decided to write it up and present it to the group for discussion with the hope of gaining new insight into her teaching and supervision of student teachers. As she thought about writing the case, she went over the checklist of criteria and found that her case met the first four: the incident was specific to science, it had an emotional impact, she was uncertain about her decision and there seemed to be no way to handle the problem that did not cause another problem. She decided to go ahead and write her case.

Sandra's Story

Michelle and I had planned that she would teach the science lesson last Tuesday. Because planning and teaching a lesson was one of her student teaching assignments, and would become part of her portfolio, I didn't help her but I looked the plan over and approved it. She was excited about her lesson and when the children heard what the lesson would be they were excited, too.

Michelle had planned a lesson on schoolyard ecology in which the children would go outdoors and collect samples of both soil and any organisms they could find—bugs, worms, caterpillars, etc. She spent so much time explaining what they would do that the children were restless before they left the room. When they got outside, the children started running around all over the place rather than settling down to observe and collect samples. Since it was Michelle's lesson and a class assignment, I thought it best not to intervene. After a while I spoke to several children to help get them focused on the lesson. It was clear that the class was getting out of control and there was not nearly enough time in the period to finish the activity. By this time the children had also become noisy, so I spoke to Michelle and said that I thought she should terminate the lesson and start again on Thursday. She became very upset, said she was doing her best and that it wasn't fair to make her stop at this point. I told her that I was sorry but that I was in charge of the class and she had no choice but to terminate the lesson. She said OK and went into the building in tears. I got the children's attention and told them we were running out of time and that it was time now to collect their materials and move back into the classroom in an orderly way. I said that we would finish this activity another day.

Michelle returned to class after a time and continued for the remainder of the day. When school was out I asked her to sit down and talk with me about what had happened. She was still upset and repeated that she thought I had been very unfair to her. I explained that I was responsible for the children's learning and behavior and that it was clear that the activity was not going as planned, the children's behavior was getting out of hand and we were verging on chaos. She replied that I was also responsible for her learning as a student teacher and that she was not being allowed to learn.

Obviously, I am not happy with the outcome. How can I understand this incident and learn from it?

Analysis and Interpretation

The purpose of this example is to illustrate the steps in the process of writing a case. The next step for Sandra is to ask herself some of the questions listed here.

- What were my feelings as I watched the lesson take a wrong turn? What are my feelings about it now?

- Which of my values led me to act as I did? In what way were my values different from Michelle's? Or was it a question of values at all?

- Were my motives what I said they were? Did I have a motive that I didn't recognize at the time?

- Would I do the same thing again? If not, what could I do that would provide a better outcome?

- Who was at fault? Were we both at fault?

Now Sandra is ready to present her case to her group and ask for their reactions and discussion. (You, the reader, may want to discuss this case with a group of colleagues or wirh your classmates.)

Summary

The thrust of this book has been on using cases as text for studying science teaching as it is practiced in classrooms. Through reflection and discussion of cases, students may gain understanding and insights that are not readily available from studying theories of learning and procedures for conducting science lessons. Another way to learn from cases is by writing them. This chapter outlined a process of choosing an incident or situation to write about, deciding whether the case would yield new insight and self-knowledge, writing the case, reflecting on it by asking questions and, finally, discussing it with colleagues. The chapter closed with an example of a case that was produced by following this process.

References

Beyerbach, B., & Smith, J. (1990). Using a computerized concept mapping program to assess preservice teachers' thinking about effective teaching. *Journal of Research in Science Teaching, 27*(10), 961–971.

Cobb, P., & Bowers, J. (1999). Cognitive and situated learning perspectives in theory and practice. *Educational Researcher, 28*(2), 4–14.

Driver, R., Asoko, H., Leach, J., Mortimer, E., & Scott, P. (1994). Constructing scientific knowledge in the classroom. *Educational Researcher, 23*(7), 5–11.

Fosnot, C. (1989). *Enquiring teachers, enquiring learners.* New York: Teachers College Press.

Korthagen, F., & Kessels, J. (1999). Linking theory and practice: Changing the pedagogy of teacher education. *Educational Researcher, 28*(4), 4–17.

McLaughlin, M., Talbert, J., & Bascia, N. (1990). *The contexts of teaching in secondary schools: Teachers' realities.* New York: Teachers College Press.

McNeill-Miller, K. (June, 1999). Lenses on leadership: The organization as factory, family, jungle and theater. Presentation at Leadership Conference. Greensboro, NC: Center for Creative Leadership.

Novak, J. (1990). Concept mapping: A useful tool for science education. *Journal of Research in Science Teaching, 27*(10), 937–949.

Shulman, J. (Ed.). (1992). *Case methods in teacher education.* New York: Teachers College Press.

Shulman, J., & Mesa-Bains, A. (1993). *Diversity in the classroom: A casebook for teachers and teacher educators.* Hillsdale, NJ: Lawrence Erlbaum.

National Science Education Standards. (1996). Washington, DC: National Academy Press.

Shulman, L. (1993). Toward a pedagogy of cases. In Shulman, J. (Ed.), *Case methods in teacher education* (pp. 1–32). New York: Teachers College Press.

Solomon, J. (1994). The rise and fall of constructivism. *Studies in Science Education, 23*, 1–19.

Wandersee, J. (1990). Concept mapping and the cartography of cognition. *Journal of Research in Science Teaching, 27*(10), 923–936.

Wasserman, S. (1993). *Getting down to cases. Learning to teach with case studies.* New York: Teachers College Press.

Index